I is for INQUIRY

An Illustrated **ABC** of Inquiry-Based Instruction for Elementary Teachers and Schools

I is for INQUIRY

An Illustrated **ABC** of Inquiry-Based Instruction for Elementary Teachers and Schools

Bruce M. Shore, Ph.D., Mark W. Aulls, Ed.D.,
Diana Tabatabai, Ph.D., & Juss Kaur Magon, D.Phil.

PRUFROCK PRESS INC.
WACO, TEXAS

Library of Congress catalog information
currently on file with the publisher.

Edited by Stephanie McCauley

Cover design by Micah Benson and layout design by Shelby Charette
Illustrations by Juss Kaur Magon, D.Phil.

ISBN-13: 978-1-61821-987-9

Printed in the United States of America.

At the time of this book's publication, all facts and figures cited are the most current available. All telephone
numbers, addresses, and website URLs are accurate and active. All publications, organizations, websites, and
other resources exist as described in the book, and all have been verified. The authors and Prufrock Press Inc.
make no warranty or guarantee concerning the information and materials given out by organizations or content found at websites, and we are not responsible for any changes that occur after this book's publication. If
you find an error, please contact Prufrock Press Inc.

Prufrock Press Inc.
P.O. Box 8813
Waco, TX 76714-8813
Phone: (800) 998-2208
Fax: (800) 240-0333
http://www.prufrock.com

Table of Contents

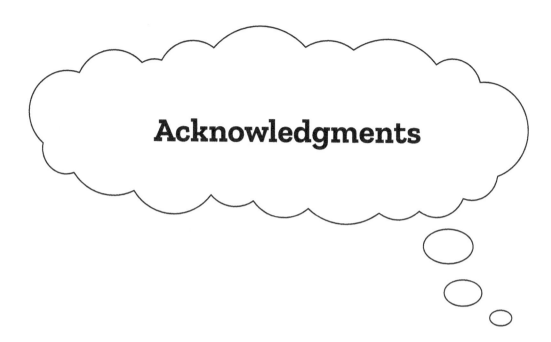

Acknowledgments

It would have been impossible to write this book without the unending support of our families and many colleagues over the decades. We especially thank the students, teachers, school leaders, and administrators who have welcomed us in their classes and schools as part of research, to share in professional development activities, and to partner in launching inquiry-based learning and teaching. We also highly value the support we have received as we brought our interest in inquiry to college and university instruction in several countries. Finally, we express special gratitude to all who read this handbook and find useful ideas to implement in their teaching.

Preface

Why We Wrote This Book

We wrote this book to collaborate with educators who value the idea of affording their students the opportunity to participate in inquiry and learn how to inquire. Because inquiry gives students learning choices, and students and teachers work as coparticipants in teaching and learning, we also find inquiry a joyful and satisfying way to give students an authentic context for using and honing their skills in literacy, problem solving, mathematics, reasoning, and social collaboration.

Creating a collaborative inquiry-based classroom is frequently and correctly perceived by teachers, learners, school leaders, and sometimes parents as a major undertaking, especially if educators try to do it all at once. Inquiry takes time for all participants, but when it takes off, it can be a rewarding and effective way to teach and learn. We assume that anyone reading this book has already expressed some curiosity about inquiry. Our goal is to get inquiry started and sustain it at a beginning and optimal level. We decided to divide the potentially big, scary task into small, friendly, chewable bites. One way to do that was to create an alphabet book, rather like *My First Inquiry Book!*

We invite elementary school teachers to use 26 core concepts of inquiry instruction. We chose one key inquiry-related word for each letter, highlighted it with an illustration, defined it, told a story about or described how it can be implemented in a real classroom, provided web resources with live demonstrations or explanations of each idea, and included suggested further reading for those who want more detail. There are certainly more than 26 inquiry words, so we also listed a few variations for each letter.

> The links to videos and other web resources discussed throughout this book, as well as downloadable versions of the illustrations, can also be accessed at https://www.prufrock.com/I-is-for-Inquiry-Resources.aspx.

Of course, we would like you to share the illustrations and inquiry words with your students. If parents ask, this handbook also provides brief answers to why each of these inquiry ideas is important in enhancing students' learning and the learning experience.

Elementary school teachers are very busy people. Therefore, this book is a selective presentation of core aspects of inquiry and relevant instructional practices. It is not an all-inclusive guide, but it is not simplistic. We provide a core inquiry vocabulary in a form that teachers can directly share with learners. Students should also know why they are learning in this manner; this sharing supports self-regulated learning. We would be delighted if our readers kept this book on their desks and each day picked an inquiry word to share with the class, working it into the lesson planning for the day, week, and next unit topic.

To effectively use this book, it is not necessary to start at the beginning and work your way to the end. One option is to start with *P is for Process* and the suggested inquiry process steps in Table 1 to help imagine a personal curriculum approach to inquiry instruction; the other chapters build on how to enact these curriculum process models. Another approach could be to start with *B is for Beginning*. Likewise, *D is for Dialogue*, *L is for Listening*, *M is for Meaning*, or *Q is for Questions* are just as good starting points as *A is for Activity*. Or choose any other inquiry word you would like to emphasize with your class, and then return to favorites as often as desired. The 26 ideas are really 26 categories of knowledge about inquiry as a process or as a set of instructional practices to choose from when planning lessons within the curriculum process that best suit students' grade level and range of competencies. Each chapter ends with a list of other chapters with closely related content; these might indicate a useful path for looking at different material.

What We Mean by *Inquiry and Inquirer*

Generally, *inquiry* means an investigation or exploration; it involves finding out something new because we want to know it, not just because we have to. We inquire about the things we have to learn because it is in the curriculum for that year. We inquire in a deliberate, systematic manner rather than by accident. An *inquirer* is, therefore, anyone who does these investigations and learns this way, at least some of the time. Critically, an inquirer is also someone who creates and sustains these kinds of learning experiences. Both learners and teachers are inquirers in collaborative inquiry classrooms.

The modern idea of inquiry in education is international and interdisciplinary. It draws from more than a century of research, beginning with American philosopher, psychologist, and educator John Dewey's (1902, 1916) emphases on strong links among democracy and participation in school and life in general. According to Dewey, a learner is actively engaged, not a sponge for information. He referred, for example, to what he called communities of inquiry (e.g., Dewey, 1938). Inquiry also builds on the work of Swiss biologist and psychologist Jean Piaget (1954), whose many contributions to understanding child development included the ideas that students create their own understanding (i.e., adults cannot push meaning into their heads) and that learners' ability to make sense of their world changes over time. Russian educational psychologist Lev Vygotsky (1978) built on Piaget's theory, emphasizing that the fundamental goal of learning is indeed to create meaning, a moving target with age, and that students learn best when they can learn from each other and engage in dialogue. American cognitive and educational psychologist Jerome Bruner (1960/1977) articulated that students need to learn any subject in the same way that an expert in the subject develops new ideas and insights, not by memorizing the end results of other people's mastery (as summarized and organized in textbooks). He offered the example of learning physics by acting like a physicist. American anthropologist Jean Lave and Swiss educational theorist Étienne Wenger (Lave & Wenger, 1991) pointed out the importance of communities of practice; this links with Dewey's idea of communities of inquiry. Inquiry is partly an individual enterprise, but it is especially a social undertaking, at the heart of all modern curriculum initiatives and at the core of curricula in most countries and regions that excel in international comparisons of educational outcomes.

What Makes Inquiry Unique?

Inquiry happens in learning:

▸ when students share with the teacher, to varying degrees, the role of deciding what will be learned and how (formally called co-construction of goals and curriculum);
▸ when some of the learning is based around students' interests, curiosity, and questions, not only the prescribed curriculum; and
▸ when the learning is collaborative.

By *collaborative*, we mean that at least some of the learning is done in groups and everyone's input is important to the outcome. Collaborative learning is different from cooperative learning in which much or all of the required work can be divided up and students can separate, do their separate tasks, and then assemble their work. Sometimes collaborative and cooperative work can be combined, but it is still important to change the pace and teaching methods to achieve different goals. Everyone can use a mental break and enjoy, for example, having a good story read to them.

Inquiry classrooms look and feel different from traditional classrooms. The following are eight components we could spot in the first few minutes in a classroom that imply inquiry in action. They are, to varying degrees, common qualities of inquiry classrooms:

▸ **Physical setting:** The classroom is set up with clusters of tables at which students can work together, interest centers, places for students to display their inquiry products (e.g., bulletin boards, tablets), and quiet corners for reading or reflection. The teacher is moving around the class.
▸ **Materials:** Students are not working their way through a textbook or worksheets but have access to a variety of copies of original materials, measuring or other laboratory tools, maps, field trips, guests, or even dress-up materials for different occupations. Different kinds of student products are on display. (Nearly identical orange pumpkins crayoned on paper plates and pinned to the bulletin board do not convey an inquiry-based unit on the meaning of Halloween.)

- **Dialogue:** There is small-group and whole-class on-task dialogue among the students and with the teacher. Students question and respond to each other and the teacher.
- **Academic content:** The subject matter goes beyond basics, reaches beyond the set curriculum, and makes connections across subjects. Some of the content is initiated by students' interests and curiosities.
- **Learning goals:** Principal learning units address more than content, concepts, or skills. They include giving reasons or evidence for claims, connecting big ideas, using divergent and creative thinking, and engaging in self-reflection.
- **Activities:** Beyond problems from textbooks and answering teachers' questions, students are engaged in a wide range of activities that can include artistic expression, doing experiments or projects, observing nature, journal writing, keeping a notebook or diary, and creating and solving authentic problems in authentic settings with an authentic, intended audience.
- **Allocation of class time:** Rather than 30- to 45-minute discrete blocks on individual subjects, cross-subject integration happens in nearly every class, and considerable class time (at least an hour a week and preferably more) is devoted to extended inquiry projects that might last several days, weeks, or, with older students, months. There is a higher proportion of student talk versus teacher talk.
- **Roles:** Classroom roles have evolved from highly teacher-centered to highly student-centered. Learners do more things that only teachers used to do, and vice versa. Both students and teachers engage in more roles, and there are more diversified roles for all.

In a classroom that is beginning its inquiry journey, some of these elements will be present some of the time. The teacher and the students will be aware that they are on this journey. Both will improve and become more comfortable with inquiry with practice over time.

We want to inspire readers to try many ways of making inquiry happen in the classroom. This book provides many tested ideas and practices to choose from and apply in the classroom. Most students find curiosity about new things irrepressible. But motivation diminishes quickly unless there is a commitment to discover more. To systematically inquire about something requires more than being momentarily curious. It entails a knowledge of how to inquire and regular opportunities to be shown the inquiry process. Because learning how to inquire has many levels of complexity and skill, students need to have plenty of opportunities across the years of elementary school to do so in a safe and supportive classroom environment. Classroom inquiry looks different on the first and last days of a school year. It looks different in different subjects. And the results of student exploration and investigation on the same topic, problem, or question can look different but still be valid. *Vive la différence!*

See Inquiry in Action

Corwin. (2015). *John Hattie on inquiry-based learning* [Video]. YouTube. https://www.youtube.com/watch?v=YUooOYbgSUg

John Hattie explains that learners need to be prepared with vocabulary and other skills for inquiry (e.g., observation, note-taking) to have a larger impact. Take care that children do not delve into data-collection steps of the inquiry process before ensuring they have a well-formed conception of the research topic and, in later grades, the scope of the research question or problem.

Crombie, S. (2014). *What is inquiry-based learning?* [Video]. YouTube. https://www.youtube.com/watch?v=u84ZsS6niPc

This animated video about basic principles of inquiry-based learning starts with, "Tell me and I forget. Show me and I may remember. Involve me and I will understand." Students in inquiry-based learning construct their own understanding of knowledge by asking questions.

Murdoch, K. (2015). *What does it mean to be an inquiry teacher?* [Video]. YouTube. https://www.youtube.com/watch?v=xlX32gB_e-w

An experienced teacher describes inquiry teachers as students' partners in learning; they know how to sit with students, ask good questions, scaffold learning, and have full knowledge of curriculum.

Further Reading

Aulls, M. W., & Shore, B. M. (2008). *Inquiry in education: The conceptual foundations for research as a curricular imperative* (Vol. 1). Routledge.

Bruner, J. S. (1977). *The process of education: A landmark in educational theory*. Harvard University Press. (Original work published 1960)

Dewey, J. (1902). *The child and the curriculum*. The University of Chicago Press.

Dewey, J. (1916). *Democracy and education: An introduction to the philosophy of education*. Macmillan.

Irving, J. A., Oppong, E., & Shore, B. M. (2016). Alignment of a high-ranked PISA mathematics curriculum and the Parallel Curriculum for gifted students: is a high PISA mathematics ranking indicative of curricular suitability for gifted learners? *Gifted and Talented International, 31*(2), 114–131. https://doi.org/10.1080/15332276.2017.1356657

Lave, J., & Wenger, É., (1991). *Situated learning: Legitimate peripheral participation*. Cambridge University Press.

Piaget, J. (1954). *The construction of reality in the child* (Trans. M. Cook). Basic Books.

Vygotsky, L. S. (1978). *Mind in society: The development of higher psychological processes* (Trans. M. Cole). Harvard University Press.

Wenger, É. (1998). *Communities of practice: Learning, meaning, and identity.* Cambridge University Press.

About the Illustrations

The unique illustrations in this book were created to provide primary and elementary school teachers with a tool that is fun, familiar in form, and attractive. We wanted the illustrations to be whimsical and to catch the reader's eye, but also much more. In most familiar alphabet books, learning the 26 letters or simple words is the primary goal. The emphasis is on the letter itself, its sound or sounds, and a familiar word it begins. On the other hand, we have chosen some words that might be less familiar, or whose use might be less familiar. For example, E represents Evidence. Our goal is to emphasize the importance of evidence and evidence-based thinking in inquiry. As a result, the E was transformed into a picture of a tool for gathering evidence. Our illustrations also place the letters against a background that, in several cases, creates both a mood and space for more of the message, such as types of evidence.

I is for Inquiry

The illustrations are an integral part of the story of the book and each chapter. The cover sets the tone by emphasizing the collaborative nature of inquiry learning, which can be a bit hectic as students think and contribute, and—purposefully—there is no adult teacher in this image because the learners need to construct meaning themselves to learn effectively. But the teacher is there, monitoring what is happening in this learning group, listening to the dialogue, and creating the learning situation in the first place. In the chapter illustrations, the letters take different forms, from a musician whose guitar-like activity collection forms the cross-stroke in A, to dialoguing faces in D, a listener with a very large ear for L, and two Ns negotiating how to divide the pie (a pie example is in the text).

We invite you to look back at the illustrations while reading the material. Also, please do share the illustrations with learners as they are brought into the world of inquiry. There are several ways of sharing these. For example, can students find the letter in the picture? More critically, can they find the inquiry ideas in the pictures? Can they do so before sharing a narrative? Can they find the humor? And how would they use their artistic talents in drawing, singing, playing an instrument, or using poetry, prose, dance, or sculpture to create an image of inquiry in general or the 26 specific inquiry ideas we have emphasized?

Illustrations are intended to attract us to the content, help us remember, stimulate our imaginations, and add entertainment. Canadian sociologist and media commentator Marshall McLuhan (1960) once quipped that there is no "basic difference between education and entertainment" (p. 3). We hope our images of inquiry help to bring both together.

A is for Activity

Learning is more effective and motivating when students are active and engaged rather than passive. An activity has a learning goal or outcome, directions for what students should do and why, and a tangible product that is sometimes formally evaluated. Inquiry activities are of three kinds:

1. **Social collaboration:** Includes making instructional decisions with the teacher, choosing with peers, teamwork, dialoguing, and collaborating.
2. **Engagement in the inquiry process:** Includes finding and answering questions; collecting data by reading, observing, and writing; interpreting data; presenting findings; and learning from others.
3. **Cognitive strategies:** Include brainstorming, identifying topics and main ideas, categorizing and classifying concepts and ideas, note-taking, summarizing, asking higher order questions, and evaluating.

Making Activity Happen

We chose to emphasize one particular, powerful activity that can be repeatedly used to engage a class in initiating the inquiry process: brainstorming. Other chapters in this book present numerous options for activities, from negotiating to questioning to sharing.

All inquiry requires discovering what one already knows about the general inquiry topic or question. Brainstorming helps model this process. The topic can be based on a curriculum unit theme or a previous topic in any subject in which students demonstrate interest. The teacher announces the topic and asks the class to free-associate everything that comes to mind about the topic. Learners need assurance that free association means "anything goes." Model free association by thinking aloud and inviting students to help, which allows students to become more aware of the meaning of a topic or concept by bringing to mind words, phrases, and ideas. Students can find out how much the class together seems to know, who knows what, and how the words and ideas they already know might be connected. They can also reflect on what they might want to know more about. Brainstorming then focuses on building a shared understanding from which a central question emerges, which students will answer by searching for more information.

In primary and intermediate grades, the teacher writes the topic and records what students suggest on chart paper or a SMART Board, flipchart, blackboard, or projector. Recording must be rapid, and repeating contributions aloud allows students to check that what the teacher records is what they intended. This honors each contributor. Some paraphrasing of original free associations can help when a student is slightly off target. For example, teachers might ask, "Did you mean to say _____? Could we say this another way?"—but we should not overdo this in order to keep all students' attention.

Once the contributions of new ideas subside, teachers can ask the class to identify the most important or most general words, or ideas that other words in the list elaborate, so teachers can then put the students in groups. Sometimes grouping students with their friends (as long as no one is left out) might be more effective, possibly because these groupings allow criticism and are safer, and power relationships are less critical. Teachers can guide students to eliminate words that are irrelevant to the general topic or synonymous with another. Groups can then share their conclusions.

Brainstorming facilitates individual students relating existing knowledge to new knowledge on their own in order to start an investigation on a topic, learn more about a familiar topic, or generate a question to systematically investigate. At any grade level, initially explain the brainstorming goal and steps, and then work collaboratively. Eventually this routine helps all students internalize the steps and feel confident about brainstorming alone or with classmates.

A related cognitive strategy activity is predicting, which can be introduced even before students can independently read or write. Consider showing a book cover or illustration, reading the title, and asking students to contribute ideas of what the story is about or how it will begin. After reading the first page aloud, ask students to use this information to predict what will happen next in the story. This can be a whole-class or small-group activity. Predicting can be used in any subject. In science, we might ask what will happen if we put another coin on one side of a balance. In arithmetic, we might explore changing the impact on sums and differences if we change the numbers or, with older students, the impact on fractions, ratios, or area. Engaging in predicting as brainstorming also prepares learners to learn together to think ahead and self-evaluate their problem-solving processes before they actually delve into a specific problem.

Sustained student participation over extended periods of time (days, weeks, or even months) is a key feature of inquiry. As often as possible, activities should have a practical application and should typically address making the world a better place.

Why Activity is Important

Inquiry incorporates a wide range of activities and, therefore, results in effective learning that sticks. There is no inquiry without activity. Brainstorming and predicting are easy to implement in any classroom and any grade without special equipment. Brainstorming initiates investigation; it is an organizer for actively selecting concepts to use as search terms, and it allows students to become further informed about the general topic of interest. The teacher should initially facilitate this process with the class. Brainstorming allows the learner to focus on a general topic, become more deliberately aware of personally meaningful search terms, and look up relevant information from available resources. Results include motivation and confidence to search for more information about the general topic and to make connections among concepts and topics. Predicting sustains engagement until confirmation is eventually reached. Accurate and almost-accurate prediction enhances positive self-feelings and self-efficacy.

See Activity in Action

Edutopia. (2010). *Music and dance drive academic achievement* [Video]. YouTube. https://www.youtube.com/watch?v=ISTUqQeXPcM

Elementary schools in Tucson, AZ, animate students through the arts.

ErinWeberTeacher. (2016). *Process writing: Brainstorming* [Video]. YouTube. https://www.youtube.com/watch?v=ArT9qQC1Vsc

Primary-grade teacher Erin Weber engages students in brainstorming about "a time that I was happy." After Weber gives examples of when she was happy, the students brainstorm about the topic and share their stories in groups.

The Science Learning Hub, University of Waikato. (2015). *Making predictions* [Video]. https://www.sciencelearn.org.nz/videos/1583

New Zealand first-grade teacher Samantha Diggins starts by finding out what her students already know about the sun. She then invites them to suggest what will happen to water outside under the sun and write all of their answers. The students observe a simple experiment to test their predictions: "A guess is always right until you try to find out if it actually is right."

Ward, Y. (2015). *How to structure an inquiry based lesson* [Video]. YouTube. https://www.youtube.com/watch?v=IOWn6DZrQ40

This is an animated summary of five main steps to structuring an inquiry-based lesson.

Watson, M. (2017). *Brainstorming lesson* [Video]. YouTube. https://www.youtube.com/watch?v=GcWYRcsOfjM

Upper-elementary grade teacher Melaney Watson uses brainstorming with her students as they set out to write a story. She asks them to think about a story they read and why they liked it: "What do you want your reader to know about the character in your story?" She starts by modeling the process, clarifying meaning, and demonstrating that all ideas are accepted.

Other Inquiry Words Starting With A

- ‣ Active learning
- ‣ Alignment
- ‣ Argument (see *E is for Evidence*)
- ‣ Authenticity, authentic
- ‣ Autonomy (see *O is for Owning*)

Connections

This chapter is especially related to *C is for Collaborating, D is for Dialogue, E is for Evidence, H is for Hypothesis, J is for Juxtaposing, O is for Owning, N is for Negotiating, Q is for Questions, S is for Sharing,* and *V is for Valuing.*

Further Reading

Alvarado, A. E., & Herr, P. R. (2003). *Inquiry-based learning using everyday objects: Hands-on instructional strategies that promote active learning in grades 3–8.* Corwin.

Dewey, J. (1902). *The child and the curriculum.* The University of Chicago Press.

Ferlazzo, L. (2014). *Response: The best ways to engage students in learning.* Education Week. https://blogs.edweek.org/teachers/classroom_qa_with_larry_ferlazzo/2014/12/response_the_best_ways_to_engage_students_in_learning.html

Graham, K. (n.d.). *Brainstorming activities* [Collection]. Pinterest. https://www.pinterest.com/karimgraham/brainstorming-activities

McNair, A. (2019). *A meaningful mess: A teacher's guide to student-driven classrooms, authentic learning, student empowerment, and keeping it all together without losing your mind.* Prufrock Press.

The University of New South Wales, Sydney. (2016). *Brainstorming.* https://teaching.unsw.edu.au/brainstorming

B is for Beginning

Every adventure begins somewhere. The first step can be the hardest. American author Chauncey Depew said, "The first step towards getting somewhere is to decide that you are not going to stay where you are." Moving to inquiry teaching is such a decision. Portuguese soccer goalkeeper and coach Nuno Espirito Santo added, "If you embrace a project that will require time and patience, then you need something to work on. So the first step of the project is to create an identity." This chapter is about first steps toward inquiry teaching and the importance of comfortably self-identifying as an inquirer and inquiry teacher.

Making Beginning Happen

We talked with teachers in an elementary school that had committed to becoming inquiry-based. We requested past lesson examples that perhaps included inquiry. The physical education teacher believed his responsibility for students' physical safety required close control, but he recalled a successful class in which he prepared different sizes and shapes of balls. He divided the students into teams, asked each group to select one ball, invent a game, and then play their game. "Was that inquiry?" he asked. Yes, indeed! After hearing this, his teacher identity shifted. The following list of ways to begin inquiry and become an inquiry teacher highlights parts of this teacher's lesson:

▸ **Give students choices:** Invite students to make choices in all subjects—for example, about materials to work with, topics to address, or which story character most interests them. Choices create ownership of the content and methodology. In inquiry, this is called co-constructing the curriculum.

▸ **Have students work in small groups:** Jointly draft some basic rules (e.g., listening respectfully and taking turns). Group work enables collaboration, negotiation, and communication skills.

▸ **Promote student-student dialogue:** This can be helpful to achieve a goal that is attractive to students—in this case, invent a game—but the focus can be a poster announcing an event, a current events bulletin, a story ending, a topic of search for information, etc.

▸ **Incorporate games into learning:** Games, mathematical teasers, adapted TV shows such as *Jeopardy*, or picture puzzles can integrate physical activity, fun, and interaction. *Where in the World Is Carmen Sandiego?* can impact reading and geography, as well as encourage social interaction. Snakes and Ladders can reinforce arithmetic operations, number facts, and turn-taking. Students can invent games that achieve similar goals, also linking creative and artistic talents.

Another first inquiry step is reading a story but stopping before the end. Ask how the story could or should end, and then delegate the conversation to small groups. Students can share their conclusions orally or in writing. Even the familiar show-and-tell, in which students describe interesting things they have read, heard, or seen, can invoke curiosity and dialogue about implications.

Ask students for their questions about any topic that they choose or that you select. They can help decide what to examine first or next. Having students dictate or write this list builds ownership for the learning. Elementary school students can handle different but acceptable ways to decide who speaks next, decorate a room, plan a garden, build a block tower, assemble a picture puzzle, or solve a mathematical, scientific, literary, or social problem. The underlying idea is to shift from 100% teacher direction to shared responsibilities. Rather than waiting (patiently or not) for their teacher to give directions for the lesson, students come into the classroom and get right to work.

There are many kinds of classroom inquiry. To begin, think of three broad types that move from teacher-driven to student-driven:

- ▸ **Guided inquiry:** The teacher chooses the topic, assembles resource materials (e.g., interest centers), gives detailed instructions about how to proceed, and evaluates the outcomes.
- ▸ **Project-based inquiry:** The teacher usually guides and approves the topics and each step of a working plan, and evaluates the outcome. Some form of sharing (e.g., essay, presentation, video, poster) concludes the project. (*Note.* Students should initially undertake this kind of inquiry for short time periods.)
- ▸ **Discovery-driven inquiry:** Students' interests especially drive choices. Learners are responsible for most or all of the planning and execution of a project over several days, weeks, or months. Students play a central role in evaluating progress and the ultimate outcomes.

Students and teachers can slowly move up this progression, building trust in their respective ability to tackle more complex inquiry.

Beginning inquiry should be small and exploratory, even just a few minutes of one class. Over weeks or months, it can be used more often, in more depth, and with increased student leadership, but never totally out of the teacher's oversight. Gradually, you will build a collection of teaching ideas, classroom resources, and experiences that have worked for you or for others, building your confidence as an inquiry teacher and your students' confidence as inquiry learners.

Why Beginning is Important

First experiences need to be successful and enjoyable. This attracts both teachers and students. Successes reassure teachers that they can simultaneously achieve general curricular goals (in particular, for content coverage—see *E is for Evidence* for an example) and commit to inquiry-based teaching. A comfortable, achievable, confident first step begins the inquiry journey, even to a challenging destination: "I am an inquirer. I am an inquiry teacher."

See Beginning in Action

Edmonton Regional Learning Consortium. (2016). *Inquiry in social studies –
A lesson from grade one* [Video]. YouTube. https://www.youtube.com/watch
?v=vIvcIw04M74

The task is to select landmarks in Edmonton, Alberta, to show a visitor.
The teacher helps students begin making choices, empowers them to search for
what interests them, gives frequent positive feedback, and calls for students to
reflect on their thinking. She asks, "How is this project making us think?" and
"Have you changed your thinking . . . ideas?"

Spencer, J. (2017). *What is inquiry-based learning?* [Video]. YouTube. https://
www.youtube.com/watch?v=QlwkerwaV2E

Clips from the Harry Potter movies show Harry as a beginning inquirer and
then starting his own school to pursue his interests. The video includes a history of the origins of inquiry-based learning and how to start inquiry teaching.
Teachers need to help students ask great questions, find the answers, and share
their results with their peers.

Other Inquiry Words Starting With B

- Bolster (support, strengthen)
- Brio (gusto, enthusiasm)
- Brown, Ann (see *D is for Dialogue*)
- Bruner, Jerome (see *E is for Evidence*)

Connections

This chapter is especially related to *A is for Activity*, *I is for Interests*, *S is for
Sharing*, *T is for Talk Time*, and *V is for Valuing*.

Further Reading

Colburn, A. (2000). An inquiry primer. *Science Scope, 23*(6), 42–44. https://
www.jstor.org/stable/43180086
Daniels, H. (2017). *The curious classroom: 10 structures for teaching with student-
directed inquiry*. Heineman.

C is for Collaborating

Collaborating is what the members of a class, as a learning community, do to construct meaning together and share the meanings accomplished by reaching inquiry learning goals. A learning community is directed toward learning in a constructivist, social environment. Collaborating requires involving all group members in every key step of a project, whereas cooperating allows each person to make an independent contribution. Collaborating involves everyone interacting, sharing ownership of the process as well as the final outcome, and generating shared meaning of the main ideas.

Making Collaborating Happen

We observed an upper elementary class preparing for a trip to the moon—in their classroom! They decided what tasks were essential and who would do what (through job applications). Tasks included building a spaceship from cardboard, planning and equipping scientific experiments to conduct on the moon and during the voyage, creating communications between the crew and mission control, and coordinating food, trips to the washroom, and wake-up calls. Parents and teachers watched the whole operation on chairs at the back of the room while the expedition was conducted. Every student was part of the decision making and planning. Groups working on each task coordinated with other groups and the flight crew as each step was developed. The teacher launched the activity by suggesting the theme, and the rest was a student adventure.

Collaborating enables students to share in the social and cognitive aspects of the inquiry process. Positive interdependence among students is key to both collaborative and cooperative learning. Social processes are necessary to student participation, but not sufficient for them to learn how to inquire as well as acquire memorable new academic content. A collaborator is a teammate or a coinvestigator during the time needed to complete a project as a class or in small groups. The collaborative learning community must be scaffolded by the teacher; this is how the teacher principally collaborates with students. The scaffold is a temporary support that the teacher shapes by designing phases of projects and relevant strategy activities, engaging in dialogue with students, and encouraging them to dialogue with each other as a means to support joint efforts to inquire (see *Z is for ZPD*).

A jigsaw approach within inquiry nicely illustrates the process of collaborating to learn. It also potentially shows how collaborating is different from cooperating. Jigsaw is one of the most highly successful instructional practices in elementary school that correlates highly with student achievement. Jigsaw can be adapted to either topic-driven or question-driven inquiry. For example, suppose that we wanted to engage a class in a project to answer the question: Why and how are beluga whales becoming extinct? As a prelude to beginning the jigsaw, a brainstorming session can help assure a shared base of knowledge of the core concepts. This question about belugas could be investigated through jigsaw in small groups instead of individually.

The following are basic steps for using a jigsaw to enable collaboration. Steps 1–3 could be collaborative if the students work as a class or in groups. If students participate in choosing groups, they need to ensure that no one in the class is left out:

1. Select one general topic or question for the class to research.
2. Divide the general topic or question into subtopics that elaborate the general topic.
3. Divide the class into groups with as many students as the number of subtopics. Try to keep group size at four or five students.

4. One member of each group becomes responsible for researching a subtopic.
5. Each student meets with students from other groups who are researching the same subtopic. Students search together for information to answer the general topic or question.
6. Each member of the subtopic group then returns back to their original group to explain and illustrate to each other what they have learned.
7. Either stop jigsaw after Step 6 or lead a whole-class discussion to comment on subgroup findings. Invite further student questions and discussion, and help students connect any of the big ideas not yet identified by subgroups.

If, at Step 4, students set off to explore the subtopics individually, this would be cooperation. Jigsaw becomes genuine collaboration in Steps 5–7 when the teacher repeatedly facilitates groups, and then the whole class, as communities of inquirers in making sense of the results reported. Through dialogue, the teacher guides students to share in identifying and connecting the subtopics to the general topic. This empowering experience allows the groups and class to co-construct possibilities for deeply understanding the general topic and how subtopics contribute to the general topic.

Why Collaborating is Important

The world's complex problems are rarely solved by individuals in isolation. Twenty-first century occupations demand collaboration skills. Collaborative inquiry experiences involve students in the challenge of creating an organized body of knowledge over increasingly extended periods of time. The teacher actively and repeatedly facilitates overcoming the gaps between what students know and what they need to know. Reflecting on and presenting new knowledge would be overwhelming without collaboration. Collaboration builds meaning out of isolated information and brings pride and joy into the learning experience.

See Collaborating in Action

Kerkhoff, S. (2019). *Jigsaw collaborative learning strategy* [Video]. YouTube. https://www.youtube.com/watch?v=JGLLhlkuaOg

This video provides a detailed explanation and diagrams of the jigsaw method.

Reading Rockets. (2012). *Jigsaw* [Video]. YouTube. https://www.youtube.com
/watch?v=mtm5_w6JthA

This video shows a graphic representation of using a jigsaw strategy. Then, the teacher, Kathy Doyle, and her students show how the strategy works in action in a real classroom with explanations, questions, and answers.

Wufei87. (2018). *Cooperative vs collaborative* [Video]. *YouTube*. https://www.
youtube.com/watch?v=uwvtfYa169k

This short animation covers constructivism and similarities and differences between cooperative and collaborative learning. These terms are often used interchangeably, although they are not exactly the same.

Other Inquiry Words Starting With C

- Case-based and project-based learning
- Causal thinking
- Challenge
- Co-construction of knowledge or meaning
- Collaborating
- Collecting and analyzing data (see *S is for Sharing*)
- Comfort with ambiguity and ill-defined/open-ended questions
- Communicating findings
- Community
- Compare and contrast (see *J is for Juxtaposing*)
- Complement
- Connecting to prior knowledge (see *I is for Interests* and *M is for Meaning*)
- Creativity, creating knowledge
- Critical thinking

Connections

This chapter is especially related to *D is for Dialogue*, *L is for Listening*, *N is for Negotiating*, *R is for Roles*, and *S is for Sharing*.

Further Reading

Abrami, P. C., Chambers, B., Poulsen, C., De Simone, C., Apollonia, S., & Howden, J. (1995). *Classroom connections: Understanding and using cooperative learning*. Harcourt Brace.

Aronson, E., & Patnoe, S. (1997). *The jigsaw classroom: Building cooperation in the classroom* (2nd ed.). Longman.

Brown, A. L. (1992). Design experiments: Theoretical and methodological challenges in creating complex interventions in classroom settings. *The Journal of the Learning Sciences, 2*(2), 141–178. https://doi.org/10.1207/s15327809jls0202_2

Gillespie, A., & Richardson, B. (2011). Exchanging social positions: Enhancing perspective taking within a cooperative problem solving task. *European Journal of Social Psychology, 41*(5), 608–616. https://doi.org/10.1002/ejsp.788

Hattie, J. (2012). *Visible learning for teachers: Maximizing impact on learning*. Routledge.

Law, Y.-K. (2010). The effects of cooperative learning on enhancing Hong Kong fifth graders' achievement goals, autonomous motivation and reading proficiency, *Journal of Research in Reading, 34*(4), 402–425. https://doi.org/10.1111/j.1467-9817.2010.01445.x

Nokes-Malach, T. J., Zepeda, C. D., Richey, J. E., & Gadgil, S. (2019). Collaborative learning: The benefits and costs. In J. Dunlosky & K. Rawson (Eds.), *The Cambridge handbook on cognition and education* (pp. 500–527). Cambridge University Press.

Pai, H.-H., Sears, D. A., & Maeda, Y. (2014). Effects of small-group learning on transfer: A meta-analysis. *Educational Psychology Review, 27*(1), 79–102.

Souvignier, E., & Kronenberger, J. (2007). Cooperative learning in third graders' jigsaw groups for mathematics and science with and without questioning training. *British Journal of Educational Psychology, 77*(4), 755–771. https://doi.org/10.1348/000709906X173297

Williams, J. M., Cera Guy, J. N. M. T., & Shore, B. M. (2019). High-achieving students' expectations about what happens in classroom group work: A review of contributing research. *Roeper Review, 41*(3), 156–165. https://doi.org/10.1080/02783193.2019.1622165

D is for Dialogue

Dialogue is a rich, two-way interchange about one or more topics. It serves emotional, social, and academic goals, often simultaneously. Dialogue is more than casual conversation. Two or more participants purposefully speak and actively listen, typically to make a decision, construct new or alternative meaning, foster deeper understanding, or strengthen connections among ideas. Dialogue must include teacher-student modeling plus student-student interaction. Lessons need planned time to make this possible. Dialogue is one of the easiest and best ways to engage students in inquiry.

Making Dialogue Happen

Dialogue involves creating learning situations in which students interact to achieve a learning goal. For example, grade 1 teacher Mary promotes dialogue by showing students sitting in a circle a stimulating picture related to a monthly inquiry theme. She then asks the students to pick a partner on their left: "Take turns telling your partner all of the things you see in the picture." Mary asks the partners to decide together what looks interesting or makes them curious.

If we use this strategy with older students, pairs can write what they see on half of a page and what is most interesting on the other. Alert them to listen carefully, use eye contact, and nod their heads to agree or disagree. Disagreement is normal in dialogue. Therefore, help students disagree respectfully and politely. From these lists of what students saw and thought was important, you might ask students to predict how what others responded resembles what they saw or consider most interesting. After several predictions, discuss how students could gather information from the lists to support or challenge the accuracy of these predictions.

Teachers can initiate and model dialogue, although inquiry becomes more powerful and motivating when students take ownership. Stories, explanations, directions, elaborations, and definitions inform students about new knowledge, concepts, and facts. Students gradually recognize that their own contributions are consequential to making meaning and deciding on classroom inquiry activities and projects.

One structured dialogue approach is paired discussion. Students individually prepare by describing what they observed in a picture or chart (that could be provided by the teacher) and writing a description of what they observed and also what was most interesting. Then they work in pairs. Student 1 shares observations and asks Student 2 to try to figure out what Student 1 found most interesting. Student 2 responds. Student 1 gives feedback about Student 2's response. Then the students switch roles to repeat the exercise. They can also discuss the similarities and differences in their lists of observations and most interesting points. Learners need clear rules and teacher modeling in this approach. In lower elementary grades, the predicting part should likely be omitted, keeping a focus on comparing and contrasting. In upper elementary grades, the pair could repeat the experience with another pair and engage in the predicting part. The teacher then might ask the class, "Did your group find any evidence linking what a person chooses to describe from a picture and what they consider most interesting in the picture? Why do different observers sometimes notice different or the same things, or find them more or less interesting?"

A variation is the learning dyad. The teacher assigns or students choose a story or video. In pairs, students then briefly tell what happened in the story or video and ask questions about why things happened the way they did. Then, in pairs, they take turns sharing what happened and asking and answering the "why" questions. An exchange can last only a few minutes. Both approaches can encourage students to listen actively and ask high-level questions.

The social and academic sides of classroom dialogue are inseparable. For example, trust arises from accepting others' statements. Respect softens differences, and students come to value fairness and the unique qualities that others bring. Even affection arises from frequent, meaningful dialogue. This is especially important for younger students or early in the school year for all students.

In natural or everyday dialogue, how a participant "takes up" a point that another participant initiated has a big impact on how the dialogue continues. Uptake is a useful dialogue strategy. It happens when the teacher or a student responds to a contribution within a group dialogue in a manner that relates its meaning to the overall topic or main idea of the dialogue. Uptake also facilitates active listening and connecting key ideas in a lesson with what students already know. This strategy helps scaffold higher order thinking by facilitating the weaving together of different students' comments or questions to elaborate on the key ideas. The learning goal for small-group and whole-class communications is to encourage students to actively try to make links with others' thinking. For example, we might pause during a discussion and ask, "Carla, how do you think Juan's idea from a few moments ago is related to what you just asked me?" Connections can be made across any time span, subject areas, or experiences.

Here are some other ways, along with uptake, to support dialogue. Students can discuss and learn to use these, too:

- **Paraphrasing:** Restating in our own words helps us to understand and shows respectful listening.
- **Summarizing:** Synthesize to check understanding of the speaker's main points and their interconnections.
- **Encouraging:** Brief expressions show that we are listening (e.g., "Interesting!").
- **Reflecting:** Use statements that respect the impact of what the speaker says (e.g., "This sounds very important to you," or "I never realized that before.").
- **Giving feedback:** Smiles, a thumbs up, "good idea," "please tell us more," or a brief additional point of information encourage learners to continue the dialogue.
- **Labeling emotions:** We might say, "I sense you are feeling frustrated."
- **Probing:** Encourage speakers to provide more details.
- **Validating:** Acknowledge speakers' contributions to the conversation as valuable and their problems, issues, and feelings as legitimate (e.g., "Thank you for helping," or "That's important.").

- ▸ **Pausing strategically at key points in the conversation:** Something important is taking place, or will.
- ▸ **Allowing for comfortable silences:** Time to reflect is useful in defusing a tense exchange (e.g., "Let's think about that.").
- ▸ **Using "I" statements:** These statements indicate personal investment, not just passive observation.
- ▸ **Redirecting to deescalate tension:** Switch the topic if someone becomes overly aggressive or agitated (e.g., "Would it help to think about . . .?").
- ▸ **Discussing consequences:** Ask students to elaborate their ideas by considering what might be the effect or impact of something they suggest (e.g., "If you received a gift but did not thank the giver, how might the gift giver feel?").
- ▸ **Inviting nonparticipants:** We might say, "Judy, what do you think?" or "I think Sara started to say something; let's listen to her."

On the other hand, some dialogue behavior is unhelpful, including talking over others, interrupting, not looking at others when they speak, and inserting ideas irrelevant to the current topic. These behaviors give the impression that one doesn't care about the speaker or what is being said.

Teachers can reward use of positive dialogue strategies. These strategies promote learning achievements that enhance knowledge, skills, independence, and social responsibility in realizing inquiry instruction.

Why Dialogue is Important

Russian psychologist Lev Vygotsky (1978) pondered how students advance across Jean Piaget's (1954) intellectual development stages. Vygotsky realized that social interaction was the catalyst. Vygotsky added to Piaget's idea of constructivism—in which learners construct meaning for themselves—to create the notion of social constructivism: Intellectual advancement extended beyond individuals to collaborators through dialogue. Vygotsky realized that dialogue was the key. Dialogue with others, and even occasionally self-dialogue, encourages active listening, sharing, creating, and connecting ideas. Dialogue is essential to general intellectual development and deep learning in classrooms. Participating in dialogue also gives learners a sense that they can impact their world (i.e., agency).

See Dialogue in Action

ConceptuaMath. (2013). *Rich classroom discussions in math* [Video]. YouTube. https://www.youtube.com/watch?v=n0_xDd5UyAU

Deborah Hancock's grade 4 students in Georgia (United States) use dyadic dialogue to enhance their mathematics learning. Also illustrated are students justifying their statements and explaining concepts to each other.

Edutopia. (2019). *60-second strategy: Traverse talk* [Video]. YouTube. https://www.youtube.com/watch?v=iUaPYSBi6pI

British third-grade teacher Anna Cook facilitates children's dialogue skills and confidence by having them debate topics with different partners.

Grigg, J. (2016). *Paired discussion* [Video]. YouTube. https://www.youtube.com/watch?v=bFZXDanSlwY

British upper-elementary teacher Jeremy Grigg guides students through paired dialogue with new partners every few minutes.

WatergrassElementary. (2014). *Great debate—Facebook for kids yes v no* [Video]. YouTube. https://www.youtube.com/watch?v=gsYUKRuphQI

Florida students practice debating a topic of their choice: Should children have a Facebook page?

Other Inquiry Words Starting With D

▸ Dewey, John (see *A is for Activity*)
▸ Differentiate
▸ Discover
▸ Discuss and discussion

Connections

This chapter is especially related to *C is for Collaborating, E is for Evidence, J is for Juxtaposing, L is for Listening, M is for Meaning, N is for Negotiating, Q is for Questions, R is for Roles, S is for Sharing, T is for Talk Time,* and *Z is for ZPD.*

Further Reading

Barbules, N. C. (1993). *Dialogue in teaching: Theory and practice.* Teachers College Press.

Bell, C. V. (2013). Uptake as a mechanism to promote student learning. *International Journal of Education in Mathematics, Science and Technology, 1*(4), 217–229. https://files.eric.ed.gov/fulltext/ED548246.pdf

Brown, A. L., & Campione, J. C. (1994). Guided discovery in a community of learners. In K. McGilly (Ed.), *Classroom lesson: Integrating theory and practice* (pp. 229–270). MIT Press.

Green, J. L. (1997). Jointly constructed narratives in classrooms: Co-construction of friendship and community through language. *Teaching and Teacher Education, 13*(1), 17–37. https://doi.org/10.1016/S0742-051X(96)00049-2

Hulstijn, J., & Maudet, N. (2006). Uptake and joint action. *Cognitive Systems Research, 7*(2–3), 175–191. https://doi.org/10.1016/j.cogsys.2005.11.002

Mercer, N. (2003). *The guided construction of knowledge: Talk amongst teachers and learners.* Multilingual Matters. (Original work published 1995)

Nuthall, G. (2007). *The hidden lives of learners.* NZCER Press.

Schermerhorn, S. M., Goldschmid, M. L., & Shore, B. M. (1975). Learning basic principles of probability in student dyads: A cross-age comparison. *Journal of Educational Psychology, 67*(4), 551–557. https://doi.org/10.1037/h0077001

Vygotsky, L. S. (1978). *Mind in society: The development of higher psychological processes* (Trans. M. Cole). Harvard University Press.

Wells, G. (1999). *Dialogic inquiry: Toward a sociocultural practice and theory of education.* Cambridge University Press.

E is for Evidence

"How do we know that?" Evidence consists of the defensible reasons used to conclude or trust claims about why something is true or not true. Learners can collect data, witness reports, observations, objects (artifacts), and documents to know with some confidence that white rhinos are disappearing or that there was once water on Mars. Evidence is different from opinions, assumptions, or beliefs, and it needs to be interpreted to have meaning.

Making Evidence Happen

At our first meeting with Suzanna, an experienced sixth-grade teacher whose classroom we visited several times, she told us that normally she carefully managed students' classroom experiences. However, one day she planned a catch-up period for some students. She divided the other students into teams and dispatched them to take pictures around the school in anticipation of an ecology unit. One group showed hallway litter. Another captured a dripping washroom faucet and measured the wasted water. A third photographed the empty teachers' lounge with the lights on. Class discussion followed.

Suzanna then reviewed her unit objectives. She realized that the students had covered them all, and quickly! The young photojournalists became teachers. Their photos became evidence supporting suggestions for improvements at their school: Reduce littering, fix faucets, and turn off lights.

Suzanna had set the framework: Think ecologically and observe carefully. The photographs prompted her students to reflect upon and discuss what this evidence meant. Had the students found clean hallways, they would have made a different conclusion: Students are not litterbugs. What alternative evidence would support that? How would they collect that evidence?

Making evidence part of inquirers' lives begins with commitment to reflect upon important statements students make, asking them, "How do you know that? What evidence would convince you this is true or not?" These questions initiate dialogues critical to inquiry and creating meaning. As teachers, we must also be respectful in response to replies such as, "My mommy told me so." We can respond, "Wonderful. Are there other ways you could learn more about that? How could you learn about this if your mom or dad did not tell you?"

An interactive classroom game could follow in which students must choose a statement and gather evidence that supports or refutes it. Example statements include "Cats would rather eat meat than vegetables," "You can water a plant too much," "Nights are getting warmer," or "4 + 1 = 5." Initially, work together with students on obtaining evidence, such as using different watering patterns for two flowers. You can formulate evidence-based arguments in any subject, but the evidence gathered differs.

Did you stumble over "4 + 1 = 5"? It *was* a trick! This example illustrates the difference between assumptions and evidence. Mathematics is an abstract world that people created. It has basic assumptions. For example, "1 exists" and "every number has a successor" that follows it and is "1" more—so 2 is the successor to 1, 3 follows 2, and, ultimately 4 + 1 = 5. An assumption is not evidence, but the sum is true if students know and use arithmetic's assumptions.

Beliefs also differ from assumptions, evidence, or facts. Beliefs, personal ideas of what is true or not, can be evidence of what a person thinks. A wrong belief is a misconception. Consider the question: Why is the sky blue? A common misconception is that light reflects the blue oceans. But, if so, why is the sky not beige over deserts or green over jungles? Upper-elementary grade students can explore their beliefs about the color of the sky without teachers answering. What about the statement "Christopher Columbus discovered

America"? Where did Columbus land, and when? Consider the Vikings. Also, the first Europeans known to visit America were greeted by Indigenous people. What evidence supports this?

Other common misconceptions include that the seasons are caused by Earth's distance from the sun, that the color red angers bulls, and that chimpanzees are humans' ancestors. Can students use evidence to change misconceptions? It is quite acceptable to offer evidence that others have previously discovered (e.g., real Viking ruins in Newfoundland).

Students need to show that they can accurately remember evidence or facts, and clearly identify what information in a book or other source is related to their own past experiences or knowledge. This helps them ask or answer "why" or "how" questions. Class discussions can address what is meant by conclusions, arguments, and explanations, and their place in inquiry. Beliefs are more resistant to influence by evidence-based arguments. Evidence alone is not proof of absolute truth or untruth. New evidence can change one's understanding of what is true or not. When students do not have evidence to support a statement they want to make about truth or facts, they need to be honest and clear that they are expressing a belief, not something they know and can support.

Why Evidence is Important

Regularly asking learners to justify their positions in respectful ways builds important communication skills and helps initiate dialogue central to inquiry and building understanding. Critical thinking processes are needed to evaluate evidence. When students work together to sort evidence from assumptions and beliefs, they hone critical thinking skills and improve their ability to tell truth from fiction or untruth.

See Evidence in Action

Humanists UK. (2014). *"How do we know what is true?" narrated by Stephen Fry – That's humanism!* [Video]. YouTube. https://www.youtube.com/watch?v =Yk5IWzTfWeM

This British animation compares and contrasts ways that people accumulate knowledge, either from science (i.e., careful observation, forming ideas, testing them against evidences) or from supernatural revelations: "We may never know everything, but the testing of theories against evidence . . . [is] a reliable way to gain any knowledge about how the world works . . . there is no better method."

Massachusetts DESE. (2015). *5th grade English group presentations* [Video]. YouTube. https://www.youtube.com/watch?v=vvAOyVVy67A

A Massachusetts elementary teacher prepares students for group presentations with a thorough review of the steps and a rubric for students to conduct consistent, evidence-based peer evaluations of presentations.

Other Inquiry Words Starting With E

▸ Empowering
▸ Emulating professionals
▸ Enacting
▸ Engaging
▸ Evaluating
▸ Expertise
▸ Explaining
▸ Exploring

Connections

This chapter is especially related to *D is for Dialogue, H is for Hypothesis, J is for Juxtaposing, Q is for Questions, R is for Roles, S is for Sharing,* and *W is for Who, What, When, Where, Why . . . and How.*

Further Reading

Bruner, J. S. (1977). *The process of education: A landmark in educational theory.* Harvard University Press. (Original work published 1960)

Elen, J., & Clarebout, G. (2001). An invasion in the classroom: Influence of an ill-structured innovation on instructional and epistemological beliefs. *Learning Environments Research,* 4(1), 87–105. https://doi.org/10.1023/a:1011450524504

Springer, K. L. (1999). The fact and fiction of Vikings in America. *Nebraska Anthropologist, Whole No. 124.* University of Nebraska-Lincoln, Department of Anthropology. https://digitalcommons.unl.edu/nebanthro/124

F is for Facilitating

Facilitating is performing any action that makes learning easier or more effective. Facilitating includes guiding, using organizers, monitoring and periodic checking, prompting, and explaining. These actions work together in different combinations during inquiry instruction. Facilitating also includes removing learning barriers, such as social isolation in the classroom, helping English language learners with the language of instruction, or filling in learning gaps for students transferring from other schools.

We once asked parents of preschoolers to accompany their students to build things with blocks and assemble a simple jigsaw. Some parents were very directive: "Let's build a fire station," "Put this piece here," or "Put that one there." Others facilitated their students' taking ownership by asking, "What would you like to build?" or "Which blocks do you want to start with?" The most frequent comments followed an act the child had initiated: "That's a great idea," or "Yes, let's try that again!" Facilitating enables inquirers to take greater control and responsibility for how they proceed. Whenever possible, facilitating is a helping hand that does not take over more than needed to encourage students' engagement and actions.

Making Facilitating Happen

In one classroom, students were taking turns making short presentations to share with the whole class about their individual or small-group inquiry projects. Their excellent written reports had already been discussed several times during small-group discussions, and they had received written feedback from the teacher. Several Indigenous students privately asked if they could be excused from this presentation. It made them feel uncomfortable to be featured so prominently. How could the teacher respect their modesty while restructuring the task so their classmates could benefit from their efforts? After several minutes of conversation, the teacher asked if they were comfortable telling a story—not sharing the results as their own achievement, but as an event they witnessed. The students were very happy to do so and did a wonderful job of telling the story of their research.

This example illustrates facilitating inquiry engagement by using organizers to frame the subtask in a culturally relevant and comfortable way. In inquiry, the teacher is defined primarily as a facilitator of student learning and a partner in that process, and less as the source of all knowledge and authority at the front of the classroom. Students, too, can and should learn to facilitate their own and others' learning. The use of dialogue for sharing, as well as support among students and between the teacher and students, is critical to achieving success with facilitation. Facilitation of inquiry prospers within a classroom climate of mutual trust, fairness, and respect.

Guiding. An especially valuable and direct facilitating tool, guiding can happen before, during, and following inquiry engagement. Before students start an inquiry project, a teacher can constrain the process (e.g., the comprehensiveness or size of the inquiry learning task), help students reword unclear questions, help them narrow down the topic to investigate, or assist groups in achieving agreement on who does what during the search for information on a topic. Guiding during inquiry includes reminding students to perform an action that they know how to do, modeling an action, and suggesting how to perform an action when needed. Guiding includes specifying steps for exactly how to perform an inquiry strategy, or later explaining or taking over the more demanding parts of an action.

Using Organizers. Organizers are the most indirect form of facilitating. Organizers frame or reveal the underlying structure of a task, using no overt directions. For example, a teacher might divide an inquiry project into a series of more manageable subtasks, for instance, by increasing or reducing the number of elements the learner should investigate, increasing the richness of the learning environment (e.g., providing more and more varied resource materials), or increasing the number of features the learner can control (e.g., redefining the task in terms of skills familiar to the learner).

Monitoring and Periodic Checking. This can be accomplished by the teacher openly acknowledging a group's visible inquiry progress and new learning, as well as students making progress visible to their peers and themselves. For example, monitoring is evident in the comment, "Group X has come up with a very interesting idea. Could we all think about it?" Another example of using monitoring to facilitate inquiry is status overviews. These summarize what or how well a learner has performed. They can recognize and encourage student decisions to use data to maintain or adapt self-initiated behavior. An example of a status overview in collaborative inquiry learning is a check sheet that indicates the roles group members have or have not taken on during a project. Using this tool indirectly encourages the less active students to increase their participation.

Prompting. Giving timed cues or reminders to a learner to perform a particular action can be helpful. Prompts can be given by a teacher or a peer, sent by text message, or provided electronically in an app. Prompts are more specific than status overviews because they tell the learner what to do—but not how to do it—at appropriate moments during inquiry.

Explaining. This is the most specific type of guidance and is intended for learners who lack the ability to perform a particular inquiry skill due to a limited or misconceived conceptual foundation. Explanations can be given either before the inquiry (e.g., as brief preparatory training) or during the inquiry on a just-in-time basis.

Why Facilitating is Important

Inquiry does not always progress smoothly, and the learning curve is typically uneven. Teachers must have a repertoire of interventions to advance how students carry out the inquiry process, with peer help as well as the teacher's. When a teacher does not facilitate the process, it places too great a burden on the students and results in discouragement and avoidance.

See Facilitating in Action

Edutopia. (2019). *Why inclusion matters on the playground* [Video]. YouTube. https://www.youtube.com/watch?v=CX5RuM3L1Ic

This teacher and specialist facilitate a grade 4 class in exploring their understanding of disabilities and inclusion as the learning goal. Students share their thoughts, partner at the playground, and reflect again.

Joseph, S. (2013). *Learning through inquiry with Kate Murdoch* [Video]. YouTube. https://www.youtube.com/watch?v=ZNLOwXVGn2M

As a guest instructor in an Australian class for grades 5–6, Kate Murdoch guides the students through a full cycle from whole-class introduction to student working groups, presentations of conclusions, and reflections on their learning.

Other Inquiry Words Starting With F

‣ Fairness
‣ Finding problems (discover)
‣ Flow
‣ Follow-up
‣ Framing meaningful (research) questions

Connections

This chapter is especially related to *C is for Collaborating*, *Q is for Questions*, and *R is for Roles*.

Further Reading

Alessi, S. M., & Trollip, S. R. (2001). *Multimedia for learning: Methods and development* (3rd ed.). Allyn & Bacon.

Janssen, J. J. H. M., Erkens, G., Kanselaar, G., & Jaspers, J. G. M. (2007). Visualization of participation: Does it contribute to successful computer-supported collaborative learning? *Computers & Education, 49*(4), 1037–1065. https://doi.org/10.1016/j.compedu.2006.01.004

White, B. Y. (1993). ThinkerTools: Causal models, conceptual change, and science education. *Cognition and Instruction, 10*(1), 1–100. https://doi.org/10.1207/s1532690xci1001_1

G is for Goals

A goal is something a person wants or aspires to do for themselves or others. Educational goals are more than directions plus destinations. Teachers know that new learning goals must be connected to past experiences and knowledge. Goals are central to inquiry because inquiry answers the question: What do we want to learn? Having goals is also motivating and creates a powerful combination of knowledge and desire.

Making Goals Happen

Goals motivate, and inquiry is goal-driven. Even tiny, personal goals can improve performance. We studied college students who slipped into academic difficulty (Morisano et al., 2010). They got back into good standing with 2 and a half hours of goal-setting reflection and writing on any topic. Teachers should, therefore, spend time discussing goals with students. These include goals for the current lesson as well as life goals, such as careers, hobbies, or educational ambitions. When introducing a lesson, explicitly describe the new skills and knowledge you expect students will acquire, and how these connect to what students already know.

Edwin Locke's goal-setting theory (Locke & Latham, 2006) affirms that having goals enhances performance. Inquiry goals need to be challenging, but not too challenging, or they might cause avoidance or procrastination. Ongoing feedback is also important because it is easy to get sidetracked or lost along the way. Mihalyi Csikszentmihalyi (1990) proposed a theory that highlights the importance of an optimum combination of difficulty and skill for each learner and situation. That balanced state is called "flow," like a musician being "in the groove."

How do students know they are on a good path toward a goal? Imagine chess players who concede a game after a few moves. They think ahead and calculate that they cannot win the game. They remember patterns of moves from winning and losing games. Such expert behavior is usually beyond young students' capability, but they can practice. Ask them to predict the next step in an ongoing task—and the step after that. Does it get them closer to their goal? For example, when students are working on writing, how will the next sentence follow the previous one? In an art project, what would students draw next? What is their mental image of the final product? When they finish, ask them to reflect back on their earlier decisions.

Another way to encourage self-evaluation is to work together with students at the outset to outline main steps and plan progress signposts or other markers they can use to break a daunting task into smaller, achievable pieces. Initially, teachers can give feedback about progress, but gradually we can encourage students to evaluate their own trajectories toward the larger goal. Telling them they are wrong can be demotivating and counterproductive. It is better to suggest, "Have you tried doing this? Would you like me to help you?" Students also need to practice constructive feedback when helping each other in groups. Students can monitor their feelings as they work toward a goal; these feelings should be positive. When students feel frustrated, suggest that they pause and ask for help, but not quit. A new smaller or nearer goal can be selected together.

How do students know when they have achieved a goal? Often it is self-evident. For textbook practice examples, answers or guidelines might be at the back of the book (but inquiry teachers do not rely extensively on textbooks). Students can consult each other or compare their work to a rubric. They can regularly ask, "Is my inquiry goal still the same now that I have collected more information? Does the group need to revise our topic or research question?" Teachers can ask, "Did the students experience flow? Were they in the groove?"

If you or students decide together what inquiry goal you want to accomplish, examining the path of the last inquiry might offer suggestions on how to reach the current inquiry goal. Sometimes young inquirers get started but then are unsure where they are in the process. Help may simply involve reminding the child that there is no rush and then asking, "What do you think comes next?" After a reply is given, reflect together on the steps in the inquiry project just completed. You might also recommend that a student summarize what was learned about both the content and how they learned: How did this learning connect with what they knew before? What went well? What could be improved? Such reflection after every inquiry project helps the students internalize the big steps of doing inquiry. It positively changes their attitudes toward future inquiry projects and challenging problem-solving tasks. It helps students understand that learning is not simply about filling their heads with stuff (information). Rather, learning is a process—a goal-supported personal adventure and investment. It is inquiry.

Why Goals Are Important

Purpose is another word for *goal*. Learning—and inquiry—should feel purposeful. Goals enable us to define directions and destinations. Suitable goals are full of purpose, motivating, and enable students to take the first difficult steps, reflect on progress, and fit new knowledge and skills into their existing repertoires. As the famous quipster and baseball hero, Yogi Berra, said: "You've got to be very careful if you don't know where you are going, because you might not get there."

See Goals in Action

Edutopia. (2014). *Grit curriculum lesson: Setting S.M.A.R.T. goals* [Video]. YouTube. https://www.youtube.com/watch?v=R9xMTGjsZPo

Grade 5 teachers Beth Perkins and Amy Lyon in New Hampshire, along with their students, discuss goals the students set in relation to five criteria: being specific, measurable, attainable, realistic, and time-bound.

Ejiofor, C. (Director). (2019). *The boy who harnessed the wind* [Film]. United Kingdom: BBC Films & Participant Media.

A teenager, whose family struggles and fails to pay the school fees, realizes his Malawi village is desperately running out of water due to deforestation. He notices the schoolmaster's bicycle dynamo, learns about pumps on his own in the library, and with ingenuity, determination, and some cunning, sets out to solve the village water problem.

JFF. (2013). *Self-assessment: Reflections from students and teachers* [Video]. YouTube. https://www.youtube.com/watch?v=CkFWbC91PXQ

Students and teachers from a junior high school in Brooklyn, NY, talk about student self-assessment in the classroom and how it can build confidence by comparing their work to a rubric. The video illustrates self-monitoring toward achieving goals.

Lee, J. (2015). *Inquiry based learning with Dot and Dash* [Video]. YouTube. https://www.youtube.com/watch?v=qDvSBo-uoBE

Grade 1 children enthusiastically learn how to program a robot. They invent a game to learn about bees, and then self-evaluate the effectiveness of their programming.

Other Inquiry Words Starting With G

- Gathering data (from several sources)
- Generating ideas, questions, problems, or hypotheses.
- Guided discovery

Connections

This chapter is especially related to *H is for Hypothesis*, *M is for Meaning*, *Q is for Questions*, *R is for Roles*, and *X is for X*.

Further Reading

Bruner, J. S. (1977). *The process of education: A landmark in educational theory.* Harvard University Press. (Original work published 1960)

Csikszentmihalyi, M. (1990). *Flow: The psychology of optimal experience.* Harper & Row.

Locke, E. A., & Latham, G. P. (2006). New directions in goal-setting theory. *Current Directions in Psychological Science, 15*(5), 265–268. https://doi. org/10.1111/j.1467-8721.2006.00449.x

Morisano, D., Hirsh, J. B., Peterson, J. B., Pihl, R. O., & Shore, B. M. (2010). Setting, elaborating, and reflecting on personal goals improves academic performance. *Journal of Applied Psychology, 95*(2), 255–264. https://doi. org/10.1037/a0018478

H is for Hypothesis

A hypothesis is written as a statement, starting with the words "I predict." In contrast, research questions are always open-ended questions, such as "What is the effect of heat on the effectiveness of bleach?" A hypothesis would state, "I predict that heat will reduce the effectiveness of bleach." A hypothesis is a suggested explanation for a phenomenon or links among phenomena. People generate hypotheses when they collect existing evidence about how things are connected. Researchers plan further systematic experiments to test if they have correctly understood the connections, some of which might be causal. For example, the now-proven fact that smoking tobacco can cause cancer began with a small amount of evidence, such as smokers showing up in hospitals with breathing problems more often than nonsmokers. Researchers formed many hypotheses about the relations between physiology and the chemicals in tobacco, and then looked for more data to support or refute the hypothesized connections.

Making Hypothesis Happen

Hypothesis is a big word, but elementary school students can learn to use it appropriately. Outside science, it can also mean a guess. However, in the sciences, a hypothesis is a prediction that arises from imagining possible, verifiable ways of testing a claim based on past knowledge, experience, and theory. When students predict what will happen next in a story, they are hypothesizing, but only in a nonscientific sense. They are making guesses because they lack specific information needed to generate a hypothesis. A hypothesis is a stated prediction. In a science demonstration, while explaining chemical reactions, we might ask students what they think will happen when we add vinegar to baking soda. We might ask why plants grow better in sunlight than in the dark. We can ask if an object will float, and if not, why? Can students make a prediction that they can explain through reason?

A hypothesis is not a wild guess or a baseless prediction. *E is for Evidence* proposed a simple test: "How do you know that?" For predictions worthy of the label *hypothesis*, ask "Why do you *ask* that?" or "What reasons can you give for your hypothesis?" The reply should address a past experience—something observed, read, seen, heard, or smelled. If students can obtain adequate evidence, others may accept their hypothesis.

A hypothesis is normally not at end in itself, but a means to an end or goal (e.g., to follow up and learn more). Students must test each hypothesis. If confirmed, they may move forward. If refuted, they should look back carefully at the evidence or theory and then revise the hypothesis in a reasoned manner. Repeat as needed. Doing inquiry based on hypotheses is intellectually challenging. For younger students, it is probably enough to ask them to research questions and offer reasons for their proposed answers. In *M is for Meaning*, we suggest descriptive research as a good inquiry model, especially in the primary grades. It is based on descriptive research questions about "what," "how," and "why." Its purpose is to promote understanding rather than to predict.

Both research questions and hypotheses are grounded in some knowledge and experience. They are stepping stones toward advancing the researcher's existing knowledge and understanding. To create a classroom community for inquiry, students and teachers work together to create (co-construct) new, meaningful learning experiences. Successful inquiry teachers pause from time to time to ask their students to reflect on and organize what they know, think about implications, imagine, plan, and establish grounds for evaluating their prediction.

Make time in as many lessons as possible to pause and engage students to collaborate in framing some hypotheses. What do they know so far? What comes next? What are the implications? What would happen if . . .? Then discuss ways to test these hypotheses.

Why Hypothesis is Important

Hypotheses are an important part of how new knowledge is created. They are the tool used by scientists to understand the natural world. Hypotheses are also tools to generate links between evidence and theoretical claims. Theories matter; they make it possible to conquer diseases, transport space travelers safely, build successful enterprises, and ensure that mobile phones work. Students cannot be scientifically literate without understanding how hypotheses are part of the scientific process.

See Hypothesis in Action

Edutopia. (2015). *Inquiry-based learning: From teacher-guided to student-driven* [Video]. YouTube. https://www.youtube.com/watch?v=mAYh4nWUkU0

Teachers and students across grades in a Golden, CO, elementary school demonstrate inquiry across the curriculum. Children test their hypotheses and document their observations.

Queensland Curriculum and Assessment Authority. (2017). *Higher order thinking* [Video]. YouTube. https://www.youtube.com/watch?v=vHa99yXJk2Y

Australian primary school students are engaged in higher order thinking: classification, categorization, and hypothesis testing. They classify objects based on whether they roll, slide, or both.

The Science Learning Hub, University of Waikato. (2015). *Revisiting predictions* [Video]. https://www.sciencelearn.org.nz/videos/1585

A New Zealand grade 1 class is guided through the process of testing their predictions about heat from the sun. The video combines the teacher's comments and actual classroom activity.

Other Inquiry Words Starting With H

▸ Helping
▸ Hypothesis finding
▸ Hypothesis testing

Connections

This chapter is especially related to *E is for Evidence*, *M is for Meaning* (especially the parts about descriptive research), *Q is for Questions*, and *S is for Sharing* (especially the parts about gathering data).

Further Reading

Deubel, P. (2017). *Conducting research-based projects in elementary grades with safety in mind*. The Journal. https://thejournal.com/articles/2017/07/26/conducting-research-based-projects-in-elementary-grades-with-safety-in-mind.aspx

Harkness, S. S., Hedge, S., & Given K. (2019). *A technology twist on a classic statistics lesson*. Statistics Teacher. https://www.statisticsteacher.org/2019/01/02/tech-twist-on-lesson

Libarkin, J., & Schneps, M. H. (2012). Elementary children's retrodictive reasoning about earth science. *International Electronic Journal of Elementary Education, 5*(1), 47–62.

Science Buddies. (2010). *A strong hypothesis*. https://www.sciencebuddies.org/blog/a-strong-hypothesis

Science Kids at Home. (2016). *What is a hypothesis?* http://www.sciencekidsathome.com/science_fair/what-is-a-hypothesis.html

I is for Interests

Student interests and curiosity are at the heart of inquiry. Interests often influence goals. When students are interested in a topic or question, they are motivated to find out more or seek answers. Interest can range from curiosity to being so absorbed in what they are doing that they lose awareness of what is going on around them. Interests reduce the burden on teachers to be responsible for decisions about finding ways to motivate students. Inquiry instruction includes finding the interests students already have as well as sparking and sustaining new interests.

Making Interests Happen

Interests are sometimes well developed but sometimes need to be generated. Resource centers and special events, from guests to field trips, can help build or support interests. Offering choices is extremely helpful. Asking about interests, directly or through surveys, can also spark students' interests. Participating in a survey can, too.

One way to stimulate interests is to directly ask, "What are you interested in?" However, more productive questions might be: What do you care a lot about? What are your favorite ways to spend time with your friends? What makes you wonder? These questions could also be used in a brainstorming exercise. Indirectly, show-and-tell and knowledge fairs (e.g., science or history) can reveal interests.

A more sophisticated way to discover individual, small-group, or whole-class topic interest is to provide an interest interview or written survey. This also teaches the useful inquiry skill of research. For a grade 2 unit on South American animals, for example, you might share the survey example from Figure 1 and introduce it with the following script:

> I would like to find out how deep your interest is in each of the four topics we discussed because some of you might like to do a project on one of them. In front of you is an interest survey sheet. It lists four topics: monkeys, lions, parrots, and alligators. For each topic, draw a circle around the face that best reflects how interested you are. For example, how interested would you be in finding out about monkeys? (*Read and point to the five choices.*) Now choose by circling the face expressing how interested you are in monkeys. (*Repeat the choices.*)

After students rate their interest in the four topics, collect the results and calculate the average for each. Then select the three topics with the highest average rating for the class. Use those topics to organize small-group inquiry. Grouping students who share similar levels of interest in a topic should increase their motivation to investigate. Student groups in which all of the members share the same similar topic interests are likely to discover more about these topics over several days or weeks. Their findings can be presented as a class report or display. Teachers could use the results of the presentations to guide a class discussion on what information made students want to know more about a topic and why, or who knows something they want to add to the information presented.

Intermediate students are more experienced and aware of the importance of other influences along with interest. These include how knowledgeable the students think they are already about the topic, how interested they are in each topic relative to the others being considered, and how easily they can get sources of information needed to research the topic. An interest survey for

Figure 1
Sample Interest Survey

Directions: For each topic, circle the face that best reflects how interested you are.

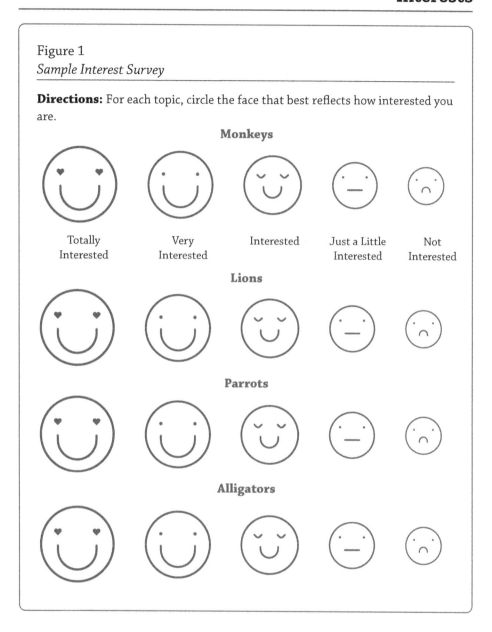

older students could give teachers more information to work with. It might look like Figure 2 for each topic.

Primary grade students are interested in most topics and questions that could be the object of inquiry instruction, but, by the middle grades, this curiosity becomes more selective. Teachers might face challenges to setting the stage for students to pursue topics of interest. It is often helpful to introduce a broad inquiry topic with a number of related topics to give choices that can be matched to individual interests. Then, we can group students together by

Figure 2
Sample Interest Survey for Advanced Students

Topic 1

1. **How much do you know about this topic?**

Nothing   More Than Most Things

[1]   [2]   [3]   [4]   [5]

2. **How interested are you in this topic?**

Not Interested   Highly Interested

[1]   [2]   [3]   [4]   [5]

3. **How easily can you get resources to work on this?**

Not at all Easy   Extremely Easy

[1]   [2]   [3]   [4]   [5]

common interests. Still, by the next day, some students lose that interest; they will not spend days reading about, discussing, sharing, or finding out more about a topic without being told to do so and seeing other students engaged.

Students may be interested in a topic but have insufficient prior knowledge to be able to access information from media or discuss the topic with others. To help, the teacher can read a good narrative story to the class or create a resource table to provide added topic-relevant knowledge. We might also begin by searching as a whole class for more information.

Why Interests Are Important?

Interests enable students to take their learning beyond the classroom and into the years ahead. Interests allow students to envision the familiar in novel ways and imagine new avenues to pursue. In some sense, students' interests also reflect their identity. Current interests channel their voluntary attention but also offer a powerful emotional pull toward new objects or topics.

See Interests in Action

Edutopia. (2016). *Interest-based electives: Engaging students with STEAM explorations* [Video]. YouTube. https://www.youtube.com/watch?v=mYfjdRWb7d0

Teachers at a Las Vegas, NV, elementary school encourage students to choose interest-based exploration classes that can be mixed grade levels. In "Toyology," for example, students explore how toys are made and invent their own.

Edutopia. (2019). *A student-driven approach to experiential learning* [Video]. YouTube. https://www.youtube.com/watch?v=x0NJx23f0iI

An Australian elementary school builds its inquiry focus around the student-centered and constructivist Reggio Emilia approach. Interests drive involvement, and multiple learning environments support individual learning needs. The school also outperforms national norms.

Storypark. (2016). *What are children really interested in?* [Video]. YouTube. https://www.youtube.com/watch?v=KW15h8aFlzY

Kindergarten children are directly asked and reply candidly about what interests them.

Wabisabi Learning. (2019). *10 exciting primary school STEM projects kids will love exploring.* https://www.wabisabilearning.com/blog/primary-school-stem-projects

This article and its accompanying videos demonstrate ways to generate interests, based, for example, on homemade ice cream, volcanic eruption, making invisible ink, the density of oranges, building a robot, and homemade slime.

Other Inquiry Words Starting With I

- ‣ Identification as an inquirer (see *B is for Beginning*)
- ‣ Imagination
- ‣ Inferences (from associations, patterns, replications, models, and theories; see *H is for Hypothesis*)
- ‣ Innovation
- ‣ Intrinsic motivation

Connections

This chapter is especially related to *O is for Owning*, *P is for Process*, and *V is for Valuing*.

Further Reading

Aulls, M. W., & Holt, W. (1988). *Active composing and thinking, level III, writer's notebook*. Kendall Hunt.

Purcell, J., Burns, D. E., & Purcell, W. H. (2020). *The interest-based learning coach: A step-by-step playbook for genius hour, passion projects, and makerspaces in school*. Prufrock Press.

Stacey, S. (2019). *Inquiry-based early learning environments: Creating, supporting, and collaborating*. Redleaf Press.

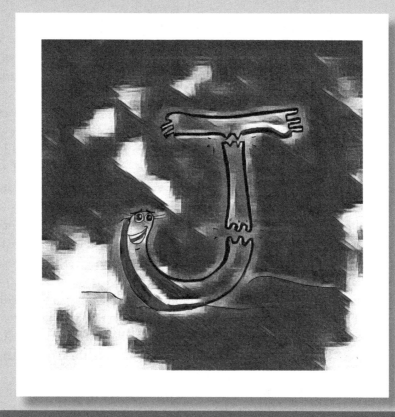

J is for Juxtaposing

Juxtaposing means putting two things—ideas, objects, characters, activities—side-by-side, physically or mentally, to observe or determine how they are similar or different. Compare and contrast asks us to juxtapose. Sometimes the juxtaposition is intended to capture our interest: "It was the best of times, it was the worst of times," began Charles Dickens in *A Tale of Two Cities*. Inquiry involves comparing and integrating new and old knowledge, and choosing among alternative questions, points of view, information, methods, and interpretations. One juxtaposition after another!

Making Juxtaposing Happen

Juxta is Latin for "right next to," and students likely already know what *posing* or *position* mean. *Juxtaposing* is a big, attention-grabbing word, like *hypothesis*, which is Greek. (That's juxtaposing!)

Juxtaposing or juxtaposition is a common literary device. For example, stories have both evil and virtuous main characters. Consider the Billy Goats Gruff and the troll, Little Red Riding Hood and the Big Bad Wolf, or Cinderella and her nasty stepfamily. Consider the porridge, chairs, and beds in Goldilocks and the Three Bears—too hot, too cold; too hard, too soft. Contemplate the two sides of Goldilocks herself, the curious little girl curled up on the just-right bed after a possible home invasion. Important concepts jump out in each of these stories. The troll is a bully. Was the violent headbutt by the biggest billy goat appropriate? Could the smaller goats have done more? Have you ever been bullied? How should people respond to bullying?

Juxtaposing occurs across the curriculum: Which is bigger, 3 or 4? How do France and Texas compare in size? Which would you prefer as a pet, a cobra or a crocodile, and why? Should you take the bus or walk to go downtown? Apples versus oranges? Right and wrong. Explain your choice. Is this story a tragedy or comedy?

Rich language and vocabulary help students address the subtleties of complex topics and understand that important topics are not understood easily. British educator James Nottingham used juxtaposition strategies to teach important concepts (Challenging Learning, 2015). In a social studies example, he asked, "What is a tourist?" Students answered, "Someone who visits another place." Was Nottingham, then, a tourist, as a visitor to their school? "No," they argued, because he was not spending money. He said that he had bought lunch. With contradictory characteristics to resolve, the students worked in groups to define what a tourist is and is not. They also learned that concepts are sometimes imprecise. In another example, Nottingham asked students if stealing was good. If not, then was Robin Hood good? Another deep conversation ensued that could similarly apply to Goldilocks. Is curiosity good? Is walking uninvited into other people's houses good? If you break someone's chair, what should you do?

Exploring a mathematics concept, Nottingham asked, "What is an odd number?" He could have accepted a correct answer of "a number you cannot divide by 2." But he pushed harder: "How could your teacher and I fairly share five pieces of cake?" These stimulating lessons are about reconciling opposing ideas and dealing with cognitive conflict. Robin Hood is a better person than the Sheriff of Nottingham (what a coincidence of names), but he stole! Students enthusiastically dialogue. They help each other generate better ideas, struggle with competing ideas, and succeed. Sometimes they disagree, or agree to disagree, at the end. Not every subject needs to be neatly wrapped, and some conclusions include unanswered questions. Creative people are comfortable living with such ambiguities. At the conclusion of a juxtaposing lesson, do not rush off. Ask students, in group discussions or individually, to reflect on what they thought their ideas were before, what they think now, and if, how, and why their thinking changed. Evidence and hypothesis both can lead to changes in our understanding, leading to learning. Juxtaposing competing ideas does so, too.

After some practice with examples, students can take ownership of the process. Teachers can frame this activity as a game. Consider show-and-tell, with students presenting news stories, reviews of what they read or watched, or other ideas. Instead of one item, have students bring two. They can explain why the items should be presented together and how they are alike or different. Explaining connections among seemingly diverse items may be a fun challenge. An unlikely or unexpected end to a story is the essence of humor. Ask the class to suggest other connections: What did students initially think were the similarities and differences? What do they think now? How did they change their minds? This activity gets complex, but capable learners love complexity.

Why Juxtaposing is Important

Juxtaposing new and old knowledge or competing ideas, and forging links between them, is fundamental to social constructivist learning. It allows students to have a voice and key responsibility in learning, to link learning to creativity and humor, and to apply knowledge in new contexts. It supports constructive dialogues and helps students learn to reflect on how and what they learn.

See Juxtaposing in Action

Challenging Learning. (2015). *James Nottingham's learning challenge (learning pit) animation* [Video]. YouTube. https://www.youtube.com/watch?v=3IMUAOhuO78

Nottingham distinguishes concepts from mere facts and illustrates how ideas can be juxtaposed so that learners can move toward eureka ("I found it!") moments.

Gracyk, T. (2016). *Charles Dickens poem it was the best of times, it was the worst of times, it was the age of wisdom* [Video]. YouTube. https://www.youtube.com/watch?v=Djz4QL-zRmc

Gracyk recites Charles Dickens's famous opening lines of *A Tale of Two Cities*, which are full of juxtapositions.

McGraw-Hill PreK–12. (2014). *How to teach students to compare and contrast* [Video]. YouTube. https://www.youtube.com/watch?v=HtGzwoVCO4E

This unusual animation demonstrates comparing and contrasting different youth novels by the same author.

Other Inquiry Words Starting With J

▸ Journal writing
▸ Judgment (part of evaluating argument and evidence)
▸ Justification

Connections

This chapter is especially related to *D is for Dialogue*, *E is for Evidence*, *R is for Roles*, and *Z is for ZPD*.

Further Reading

Balli, S. J. (2014). Pre-service teachers' juxtaposed memories: Implications for teacher education. *Teacher Education Quarterly, 41*(3), 105–120. https://files.eric.ed.gov/fulltext/EJ1078503.pdf

Barron, F. (1958). The psychology of imagination. *Scientific American, 199*(3), 150–166.

Silver, H. F. (2010). *Compare and contrast: Teaching comparative thinking to strengthen student learning.* ASCD. https://www.ascd.org/publications/books/110126/chapters/Section-1@-Why-Compare-$-Contrast%C2%A2.aspx

Steig, W. (1976). *The amazing bone.* Farrar, Straus, and Giroux.

K is for Knowledge

Building knowledge is fundamental in schooling. But what is knowledge, and how is it constructed through inquiry instruction? Students can know facts, concepts, and the relationships among them, and deliberately connect what they know with what they newly encounter. The technical term for this is declarative knowledge because the concepts can be declared or listed. Students also know how to do things, called procedural knowledge. Being aware of what they know and adjusting how they learn for the best outcome are known as metacognition, self-regulation, or metaknowledge (i.e., knowing about knowing; also called personal epistemology).

Making Knowledge Happen

Inquiry is concerned with all three kinds of knowledge. For example, students might know facts and concepts related to the environment, know how to make positive environmental changes, and be aware of what they each know and want to know more about. Teachers are also concerned about knowledge about inquiry itself and learning through inquiry. Furthermore, both learners' and teachers' knowledge are important to consider, because both groups collaborate to enable learning.

Whether learning about government, the number 5, chemical reactions, Goldilocks, or anything else, students will be more highly motivated and learn more effectively if they and teachers clearly identify this triple focus:

▸ facts, concepts, and connections;

▸ "how-to-do-it" skills related to those concepts; and

▸ what they already know and the best ways to learn more about both.

The same three perspectives apply to what it means to inquire in general and be an inquirer.

All but the youngest students are aware that knowledge is different in different subjects. Some knowledge is more concrete, concerning things students can see or touch. Some is abstract, such as numbers, caring, or concepts such as democracy. Students can learn to make these distinctions, too. This awareness helps them to feel more confident in their knowledge and to distinguish knowledge from beliefs. Just as the knowledge itself is different in different subjects, the way that experts discover new knowledge is also different; older students benefit from reflecting on how and why their inquiring might differ in different subjects. Archeologists dig and analyze artifacts. Historians look for written records or pictures, or they recruit archeologists to dig for them. Chemists analyze what happens when different elements or materials combine to make new substances or break apart. Poets and musicians explore the aesthetic senses and emotions.

Whatever the subject matter, however, the inquiry-learning process for acquiring knowledge is:

▸ **Constructive:** Learners build their own understanding—hence knowledge; our task as teachers is to create the situation in which that happens.

▸ **Collaborative:** Knowledge of all kinds is created best in purposeful interaction with others.

▸ **Progressive:** New knowledge builds on existing knowledge; therefore, explicitly making the connections is critical to learning (e.g., concept or semantic mapping).

▸ **Connected across time:** Inquiry learning is a motion picture, not a snapshot. Knowledge grows.

To be an inquirer entails accomplishing higher order learning objectives such as those in Bloom's revised taxonomy (Anderson & Krathwohl, 2001), especially evaluating. Everyday knowledge can be distorted by misconceptions, biases, and imagined realities. In contrast, inquiry-based knowledge is systematic and tested to determine its truth value based on evidence and reason.

The following inquiry teaching strategies powerfully support student learning and acquisition of many kinds of knowledge:

▸ using the jigsaw method of small-group collaboration;
▸ regularly holding whole-class, small-group, and paired discussions;
▸ using reciprocal teaching to build reading comprehension;
▸ teaching students to seek help from peers as well as the teacher;
▸ explaining and guiding problem solving;
▸ collecting and making sense of a group of concepts and ideas through categorizing and concept mapping;
▸ planning and using engaging activities and social aspects of classroom learning; and
▸ providing clear explanations and directions.

Our own firsthand observations of elementary schools that use inquiry in the curriculum revealed additional knowledge-building practices:

▸ To understand inquiry, all elementary school students should participate in the process.
▸ All elementary students benefit from learning reading comprehension, writing, and collaboration strategies.
▸ When planning the year's curriculum, teachers should organize opportunities to connect projects to one or more subjects.
▸ Inquiry-based teaching simultaneously teaches strategies (e.g., reading, writing, mathematical, and collaborative) and allows students to pursue projects over extended time, such as 1–6 weeks, and can begin with even shorter intervals with younger students.
▸ Learners should gradually engage in more and more of the roles exercised by the teacher, so everyone has more ways to learn and teach.

This rather esoteric knowledge about knowledge is not reserved for a secret society of researchers. We hope these technical terms will be used during inquiry lessons. Students can become more independent learners when they can articulate different kinds of knowledge and learning, ways of knowing in different subjects, and steps they can take to master new material and plan new inquiries.

Why Knowledge is Important

Acquiring knowledge is a goal and outcome of participation in inquiry-based teaching and learning, as with any other kind of formal learning. Inquiry knowledge lies in the process of inquiry—the concepts, interconnections, skills learned, and self-knowledge. Knowledge that can be shared, recorded, and passed on over time is part of the essence of being human (*homo sapiens*, or "wise person"). And wisdom is using knowledge and experience well in the exercise of sound judgment. A healthy society needs that every day.

See Knowledge in Action

Edutopia. (2019). *Teaching self-regulation by modeling* [Video]. YouTube. https://www.youtube.com/watch?v=UD9m5n-ZpB0

The teacher models her recognition of her emotions and how she deals with them. That teaches children self-regulation and allows them to recognize and respond to their emotions in class to facilitate learning.

FableVision. (2017). *The reflection in me* [Video]. YouTube. https://www.youtube.com/watch?v=D9OOXCu5XMg

This animated video discusses personal knowledge, acceptance, and positive self-image using the metaphor of a mirror.

LSU Center for Academic Success. (2012). *Bloom's taxonomy* [Video]. YouTube. https://www.youtube.com/watch?v=Qfp3x_qx5IM

Remembering, understanding, applying, analyzing, and evaluating are defined and illustrated with examples.

Lynn, K. (2013). *Concept map video lesson* [Video]. YouTube. https://www.youtube.com/watch?v=--oqW7FOgkM

The speaker creates a concept map (also called a semantic map) about key concepts regarding energy, but without elaboration of the links between the concepts.

MindTools. (2018). *Seven ways to find what you want on the Internet: Gathering what you need, discarding what you don't.* https://www.mindtools.com/pages/article/internet-searching.htm

This text and accompanying video compare three search engines—Google, Bing, and Yahoo—and suggest using different search engines, specific keywords, simple keywords, quotations, and minus signs to exclude unwanted results. Remember that the best hit will not necessarily appear on the top.

PK Yonge DRS. (2016). *Project-based learning: Inquiry, interest, and innovation* [Video]. YouTube. https://www.youtube.com/watch?v=WwUuBKFncxI

Procedural knowledge is illustrated in this Florida school that undertook a project with relevance to the community and value to the learners: learning to make rain collection barrels.

Other Inquiry Words Starting With K

▸ Keen
▸ Kibbitz (keep your sense of humor)
▸ Kids (the central focus)

Connections

This chapter is especially related to *A is for Activity*, *C is for Collaborating*, *M is for Meaning*, *R is for Roles*, and *S is for Sharing*.

Further Reading

Anderson, L. W., & Krathwohl, D. R. (Eds.). (2001). *A taxonomy for learning, teaching, and assessing: A revision of Bloom's taxonomy of educational objectives* (Complete ed.). Longman.

Aulls, M. W., & Shore, B. M. (2008). *Inquiry in education: The conceptual foundations for research as a curricular imperative* (Vol. 1). Routledge.

Bloom, B. (Ed.). (1956). *Taxonomy of educational objectives: The classification of educational goals. Handbook I: Cognitive domain.* Longmans Green.

Centre for Teaching Excellence, University of Waterloo. (n.d.). *Concept mapping tools.* https://uwaterloo.ca/centre-for-teaching-excellence/teaching-re

sources/teaching-tips/educational-technologies/all/concept-mapping-tools

Hattie, J. (2012). *Visible learning for teachers: Maximizing impact on learning.* Routledge.

Oppong, E., Shore, B. M., & Muis, K. R. (2019). Clarifying the connections among giftedness, metacognition, self-regulation, and self-regulated learning: Implications for theory and practice. *Gifted Child Quarterly, 63*(2), 102–119. https://doi.org/10.1177/0016986218814008

Pennington, M. (2018). *Should we teach reading comprehension strategies?* International Literacy Association. https://www.literacyworldwide.org/blog/literacy-daily/2018/07/06/should-we-teach-reading-comprehension-strategies

Pressley, M., Harris, K. R., & Marks, M. B. (1992). But good strategy instructors are constructivists! *Educational Psychology Review, 4*(1), 3–31. https://doi.org/10.1007/BF01322393

White, H. (2018). *How to construct a concept map.* Department of Chemistry and Biochemistry, University of Delaware. https://www1.udel.edu/chem/white/teaching/ConceptMap.html

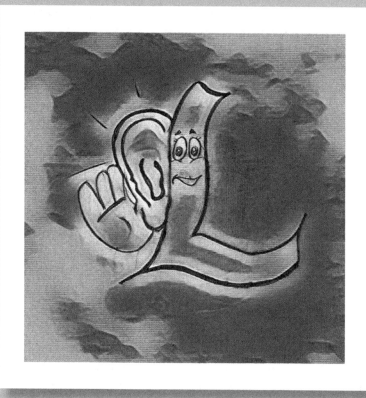

L is for Listening

Listening is part of the active process of cocreating meaning. It is more than the mechanics of hearing. Attentive listening builds rapport, understanding, and trust within a classroom. For teachers, it involves attending to and understanding students' ideas, letting students know they have been heard by giving them time to respond to teacher-initiated questions, and periodically pausing to summarize students' ideas and allowing them to check the teachers' version. Listening involves encouraging students to relate their own ideas to others' during whole-class or small-group dialogue.

Making Listening Happen

Some elementary school students are short on listening and big on letting their attention wander. Some get overly excited and mixed up when sharing their own ideas. Others might be planning what they themselves are going to say next rather than paying close attention. There is also the risk that some students do not receive listeners' attention because of interpersonal relationships or listener biases.

Actively and carefully listening helps students participate effectively and avoid forming misconceptions. Teachers who model active listening will increase this behavior among their students. Learners can figure out a lot for themselves given the chance. Practicing listening skills helps students build respect for each other's contributions, take turns, and use their fair share of the available time. It increases the expectation that they should listen and contribute. In these ways, listening also empowers students and teachers.

The listening pendulum can swing too far from exclusively thinking about one's own next contribution to being totally immersed in the current speaker's words. Listening includes trying to view things from the speaker's perspective. The goal includes listening for points of shared understanding with the speaker. This occurs in negotiating, whether as a participant or as meditator. Teachers often monitor what happens among learners and help students find common meaning.

Not all dialogue is about solving a problem. Dialogue can be playful or exploratory, for example, when students are talking about what interests or amuses them. Listening is easier in these situations, but it is especially affirming when a person briefly summarizes what was said or inserts a supporting example when it is their turn to speak. Emotions might be less constraining if students start practicing effective listening with these kinds of playful, exploratory topics.

Attentive listening, with practice, also helps the speaker clearly think and cogently present their thoughts because the listener provides feedback that they are genuinely interested in what the speaker says. By waiting until a speaker finishes speaking, the listener is more likely to grasp the big ideas. Active listening enables genuine sharing and learning.

The following are strategies to model to students from time to time, to discuss in class, and for learners to practice in order to enable active listening in the classroom:

- **Establish rules:** In a large group, students could elect a Speaker who decides who starts a discussion, how turn-taking works, and rules for fair time use, just as in Parliament or Congress. Tell students, "We all get to talk to each other, one person and one idea at a time. Without active listening, we talk past each other rather than with each other." Write the rules on a chart.
- **Listen attentively:** During dialogue, students should not try to do other things at the same time.

- **Listen respectfully:** Students must allow time and space for speakers to fully make or explain their points. Then, they should accept those points as worthwhile perspectives, but not the only ones.
- **Maintain eye contact:** This shows that the listeners are interested and paying attention.
- **Search for relationships among the speakers' big ideas:** Periodically, during discussion, have students take turns summarizing what main ideas have been shared. Otherwise, group members may leave with differing understandings.
- **Voice openly:** Show students how to share thoughts on a topic of discussion calmly and respectfully by connecting their thoughts with ones expressed up to that point. This includes asking for clarification.
- **Give positive feedback:** Learners can practice responding to each other in positive terms (e.g., "Here is one thing you said that I found very interesting. . . .").
- **Give reasons for claims and statements:** This helps everyone understand the difference between knowledge or understanding, and opinion or beliefs.
- **Be clear who "has the floor":** Whoever is speaking can hold a flag, toy, gavel, or other object that the students choose. Only that person may speak. To ask a question or make a comment before the speaker is finished requires gesturing for the object, and it is up to the speaker to yield or not. After a question or comment, the object should be returned to the speaker. When the speaker finishes, the object is handed to whoever is next. This process makes turn-taking tangible.

Why Listening is Important

Because much of inquiry-based learning is collaborative or social constructivist, listening is critical. It builds important social life skills, including concerns for fairness (such as turn-taking), respect, and inclusion. Students learn that they learn from each other as much as, or more than, from people "in charge." Active listening enables the sharing and deeper learning that comes from dialogue during inquiry projects. Collaboration and meaningful dialogue depend upon it. Students need to be able to express their understanding of concepts in their own words, be heard by others, and give reasons for their understandings in the face of alternative understandings. All of these skills support active and enjoyable inquiry instruction experiences.

See Listening in Action

EngageNY. (2015). *Teacher uses questioning techniques to engage students–Example 5* [Video]. YouTube. https://www.youtube.com/watch?v=IdP99uF9mTc

A New York teacher uses open-ended questions to introduce a geometry lesson. Students first discuss with a partner, and the teacher asks what the partner said. The approach promotes uptake and careful listening.

Ma, M. L. (2013). *How to be a good listener* [Video]. YouTube. https://www.youtube.com/watch?v=8XUE3urz3Fc

Grade 4 students recite tips on how to be a good listener: Make eye contact, be patient, do not interrupt, ask questions, relate to the topic, use positive body image, do not be distracted, be open-minded, be empathetic, and remember what people say.

TED. (2011). *5 ways to listen better | Julian Treasure* [Video]. YouTube. https://www.youtube.com/watch?v=cSohjlYQI2A

In this TED talk, Julian Treasure explains how listening works.

Other Inquiry Words Starting With L

▸ Learner-directed
▸ Lifelong learning
▸ Linking knowledge (can be constrained by lower levels of disciplinary knowledge)
▸ Linking learning experiences in class to students' needs

Connections

This chapter is especially related to *D is for Dialogue*, *F is for Facilitating*, *N is for Negotiating*, *S is for Sharing*, *T is for Talk Time*, and *V is for Valuing*.

Further Reading

Clement, T. (2019). *How to have meaningful conversations with preschoolers & pre-K children*. Rollins Center for Language & Literacy. https://www.cox campus.org/how-to-have-meaningful-conversations-with-preschoolers-pre-k-children

Glaser, T. (2005). *Summary of "Dialogic listening: Sculpting mutual meanings."* University of Colorado Conflict Research Consortium. https://www.beyondintractability.org/artsum/stewart-dialogic

Grohol, J. M. (2018). *Become a better listener: Active listening*. PsychCentral. https://psychcentral.com/lib/become-a-better-listener-active-listening

Helin, J. (2013). Dialogic listening: Toward an embodied understanding of how to "go on" during field work. *Qualitative Research in Organizations and Management, 8*(3), 224–241. https://doi.org/10.1108/QROM-05-2012-1066

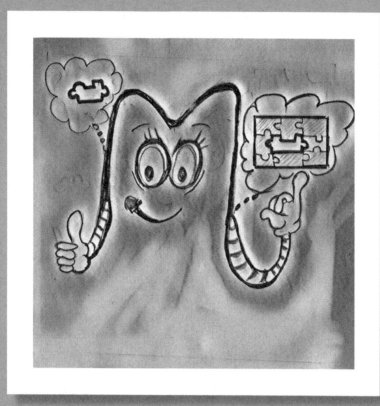

M is for Meaning

Inquiry-based instruction holds making meaning as a major learning goal, based on constructivist learning theory. Memorizing or rote learning is insufficient. People learn more effectively and productively with others. Dialogue with one or more persons is the primary means to socially creating meaning, including interrelating facts and concepts, reading and writing for understanding, and reasoning from evidence.

Making Meaning Happen

Learners create their own meaning. This was Piaget's (1954) most important educational insight. This is what makes learning authentic. Misconceptions or incomplete learning arise unless teachers build up students' repertoire of effective skills for constructing their own meaning, especially in concert with other learners. This chapter focuses on perhaps the most critical skill set for becoming an inquiry-driven learner: literacy. Literacy means not only the mechanics of reading and writing, but also using these tools thoughtfully to understand in general and to understand what is read in books or elsewhere.

Blogger Justin Lim (2010) gathered wisdom about enhancing reading skills and related classroom activities:

> When I first began teaching, I was surprised by how well my students could "read" without understanding anything. On the surface, they appeared to be strong readers, but it soon became apparent that they could not recall anything expressed on the page. . . . Although I recognized that there was a problem . . . it was hard to identify what my kids couldn't do because these strategies were skills that I regularly implemented without even realizing it. I decided to start teaching essential vocabulary while also encouraging my students to read more. But these practices just don't fully address the internalized reading strategies that are at the core of comprehension. (paras. 1–2)

The inquiry process requires reading for meaning and writing meaningfully. These skills can be applied in any subject. Based on Pearson et al.'s (1992) work, Lim shared seven ways that good readers build their understanding from written text:

1. **Activating background knowledge to make connections:** What does this remind you of?
2. **Questioning the text:** Do you agree or disagree? Does it depend?
3. **Drawing inferences:** What might be talked about next? What might happen next?
4. **Determining importance:** What do you think you need to remember?
5. **Creating mental images:** What do you picture in your head?
6. **Repairing understanding when meaning breaks down:** How can you figure out what it means? Would it help to reread to find the authors most important idea?
7. **Synthesizing information:** How can you put it all together? What is the big picture? (para. 3)

These should be frequently practiced so students can easily do these themselves as they read. Lim then added three suggestions:

1. **Thinking out loud:** Pause while reading and explain why you are doing something. Tell students, "I'm going to think out loud for a moment.

Something that good readers do is ask questions about the text. The question that I have right now is . . . What are you wondering?" (para. 4)

2. **Listing strategies:** The seven strategies shared previously can be posted on a chart. Point to each as you model it and when you praise a student for using one. The poster is a reminder to use them often.

3. **Focus on the process:** When a learner shares a new understanding or awareness, give a compliment, and then immediately ask the student to share how they came to this new insight or conclusion. You can also ask classmates to comment or add something to what was said.

We would add three more strategies to these lists, because too few students can do these well or at all: (a) write a summary sentence telling what a paragraph is about (or dictate it live or to a device); (b) identify the major topic of a selection (like "determining importance") but also identify levels of subordinate topics that elaborate the main topic; and (c) take notes while reading, with students using their own words as much as possible.

As part of inquiry projects in lower elementary grades, students can learn and practice distinguishing between a general and specific topic in a sentence. The general topic usually can be stated in a single word, such as "rain." There might be several specific topics.

Upper elementary graders can learn what a main idea statement is. The general topic answers the question: What is this about? The main idea statement is the most important statement made about the general topic. Identifying the main idea of each paragraph of several paragraphs can be tricky because the main idea often is not the first sentence of a paragraph, and sometimes the main idea is not stated at all by the author or only implied. Readers can ask themselves, "What is the most important statement the author makes about the overall topic of a selection?" The reader can then ask, "What did I learn from reading about the general topic? Which is the most important idea among all of the sentences?" Knowing how to find the general topic and main idea of any text makes note-taking much easier and useful.

All of these strategies help learners build meaning because they must slow down, pay attention, clarify what is uncertain, reread, exchange ideas, put ideas into their own words, and connect new information to what they know.

Why Meaning is Important

Inquiry demands making meaning together with others and trying to describe, question, and defend what is meaningful and how it occurs. The process and the resulting understanding are major sources of motivation for further inquiry and learning.

See Meaning in Action

Center for the Collaborative Classroom. (2013). *Making meaning grade 1 lesson videos: Guided strategy practice* [Video]. YouTube. https://www.youtube.com/watch?v=6DVBb7HRpRM

The teacher reads the poem "Balloon Man" and then asks the students to visualize it, talk to their partners about what they saw, draw what they imagined, and share the meaning they derived with the group. One child adds children to her picture because she saw the word *us*.

Knatim. (2010). *Word study in action: Activating prior knowledge* [Video]. YouTube. https://www.youtube.com/watch?v=4B3ZcDm7i-g

Students in an elementary school make predictions about the content of a new book based on the front cover and then share their vocabulary about endangered animals. This is a good example of students making meaning together and adding to each other's knowledge, with teacher facilitation.

Other Inquiry Words Starting With M

▸ Memorizing
▸ Mentoring
▸ Metacognition
▸ Methodology (see *P is for Process*)
▸ Modeling (or demonstrating)
▸ Monitoring (self-regulation, executive processes)
▸ Motivating (see *I is for Interests*)

Connections

This chapter is especially related to *A is for Activity, D is for Dialogue, E is for Evidence, K is for Knowledge, Q is for Questions, S is for Sharing, W is for Who, What, When, Where, Why . . . and How,* and *Z is for ZPD.*

Further Reading

Denton, C., Bryan, D., Wexler, J., Reed, D., & Vaughn, S. (2007). *Effective instruction for middle school students with learning difficulties: The reading teacher's sourcebook.* University of Texas System/Texas Education Agency. https://www.meadowscenter.org/files/resources/_RTS_Complete.pdf

Ericsson, K. A., & Simon, H. A. (1993). *Protocol analysis: Verbal reports as data* (Rev. ed.). MIT Press.

Gear, A. (2018). *Powerful understanding: Helping students explore, question, and transform their thinking about themselves and the world around them.* Pembroke.

Gonzalez, J. (2018). *Note-taking: A research roundup.* Cult of Pedagogy. https://www.cultofpedagogy.com/note-taking

Hippie, D. (n.d.). *Grades 6–8: Activities to teach note-taking.* Scholastic. https://www.scholastic.com/teachers/articles/teaching-content/grades-6-8-activities-teach-note-taking

Juraschka, R. (2019). *4 reciprocal teaching strategies to use.* Prodigy. https://www.prodigygame.com/blog/reciprocal-teaching

Lim, J. (2010). *Strategies for building reading comprehension.* Scholastic. https://www.scholastic.com/teachers/blog-posts/justin-lim/reading-and-thinking-strategies-for-building-reading-comprehension

Lord, K. M. (2015). Determining the main idea: Instructional strategies that work. *Kappa Delta Pi Record, 51*(3), 138–142. https://doi.org/10.1080/00228958.2015.1056669

Osler, J. (1994). Semantic maps in the primary school. *Peel Seeds, 26,* 4. http://www.peelweb.org/admin/data/articles_bogus/az0004.htm

Pearson, P. D., Roehler, L. R., Dole, J. A., & Duffy, G. G. (1992). Developing expertise in reading comprehension. In S. J. Samuels & A. E. Farstrup (Eds.), *What research has to say about reading instruction* (2nd ed., pp. 145–199). International Reading Association.

Richardson, F. (n.d.). *Reciprocal teaching: Reading and learning strategy.* National Behaviour Support Service. https://www.nbss.ie/sites/default/files/publications/reiciprocal_teaching_strategy_handout__copy_2_0.pdf

Scott, B. E. (2020). *Concept-based instruction: Building curriculum with depth and complexity.* Prufrock Press.

Shanahan, T. (2020). *Does "modeling" have a place in high-quality literacy teaching?* Reading Rockets. https://www.readingrockets.org/blogs/shanahan-literacy/does-modeling-have-place-high-quality-literacy-teaching

Stanley, T. (2018). *Authentic learning: Real-world experiences that build 21st-century skills.* Prufrock Press.

N is for Negotiating

Negotiating is a kind of dialogue that deserves specific mention. Dialogue can begin with agreement, disagreement, curiosity, or some neutral topic. However, negotiating usually begins with participants in disagreement over either the substance or process. Agreeing to disagree is a possible outcome but rarely anyone's first choice. Negotiating might include deciding how to share something of value, from dividing a pie to deciding who gets the bigger bedroom, or bargaining for a better price, allowance, or test grade. Negotiating also happens in contract bargaining, conflict resolution, mediation, and arbitration.

Making Negotiating Happen

Sometimes dialogue starts with fundamental disagreement. Students encounter these disagreements at home, in the schoolyard, and in the classroom, and they understand that lose-lose outcomes hurt everyone.

We observed four students in grades 5–6 doing a guided inquiry project together about government structures. The central goal was having students understand that how governments are organized affects the lives of citizens, and vice versa. Questions such as "What do governments do with taxes they collect?" helped the students focus. During a group activity to plan a class presentation on the information they had gathered about the successes of a particular leader, two students argued about who would present. One asserted, "I saw it first. Write something else." Another said to a classmate, "It's impossible to work with you." The teacher called for a pause and initiated a class discussion about students' roles as group members versus individuals, and what compromising means. In another incident, one student removed another student's name from a group activity because she felt that she alone had done all of the work. Another burst out, "It's about the Tory members of Parliament? Okay. Why couldn't you just tell me that?" The classmate responded, "I was going to, but you talked over me while I was about to say something."

It is useful and important to teach and practice negotiating skills and dispositions before putting learners in situations in which they will need them. Some relevant skills include understanding the meaning of evidence and critical discussion, separating evidence and facts from opinions, disagreeing civilly, giving reasons to support assertions and claims, and building a repertoire of tools for presenting and discussing observations, answers to research questions, and proposed solutions to problems.

Negotiating skills can sometimes be learned through games. The "Orange Game" by Mary Rowe (n.d.), who teaches negotiation at MIT, is for students ages 8–13. It requires one orange and about a half hour. (See Further Reading at the end of this chapter for detailed instructions.) After dividing one group in half, each gets separate goals—to get the whole orange for juice or the peel to bake a cake. Groups can comprise up to half of the class. The goal is to obtain the orange without any violent action. The groups sit in lines facing each other, and one orange is placed between them. The game gets even more tense should one person leap up and grab the orange! A debriefing period follows during which the multiple solutions can be reviewed. The students come up with most of these solutions. Debriefing can be prompted with questions about what happened, why communication is important when trying to resolve a conflict, why people might or might not communicate effectively, how they can be helped to do so, and what their own prior experiences are with such situations.

Some guidelines that can be addressed in developing negotiating ability, in planned experiences or as the need arises, include:

- no stealing, cheating, or lying;
- no physical violence;
- listen carefully to what each side is trying to achieve;
- distinguish optimum and maximum outcomes in a negotiation (maximum means getting everything you want in the negotiation; optimum means getting enough to enable all participants to experience the best possible outcome, which is likely less than the maximum for everyone);
- switch roles and take the other's perspective;
- be polite and respectful; and
- take turns.

Teachers can also use role-play and read stories about how conflicts are resolved.

Elementary school teacher John Hunter developed an elaborate geopolitical game in which students independently develop negotiating skills (see the examples in See Negotiating in Action). Several classroom sequences are shown in his TED Talk. Providing opportunities to co-construct learning experiences using an inquiry approach can reduce the teacher's need to be the font of knowledge and enhance student learning and buy-in.

Why Negotiating is Important

Negotiating is a valuable life skill. Interactions are rarely perfect. Occasionally, disputes resolve themselves. Some students, especially the highly able, enjoy friendly sparring with neither side giving in. Students individually and collectively benefit from resolving disputes, finding optimal solutions, and working cordially and effectively with other people, including some they might not choose as friends. Inquiry activities place students in situations that can easily evoke disagreements. Students can and should acquire competencies and confidence in how to resolve these disagreements through negotiation.

See Negotiating in Action

C-VILLE Weekly. (2007). *John Hunter explaining his World Peace Game* [Video]. YouTube. https://www.youtube.com/watch?v=iOC0mrmIjHo

This grade 4 teacher created this simulation game 30 years ago. Four different countries face conflict, and students have to figure out how to maintain world peace without combat as much as possible.

Edutopia. (2011). *Peace helpers become classroom problem solvers* [Video]. YouTube. https://www.youtube.com/watch?v=RhF3WgFjT88

Students in grades 4 and 5 in New York City participate in a conflict resolution program in which they also help students in younger grades solve disputes in their classrooms.

Edutopia. (2012). *Students learn the skill of conflict resolution in a multi-age class* [Video]. YouTube. https://www.youtube.com/watch?v=DazLm-VB-Ik

In this Washington state elective class, students from every grade come together to discuss and resolve their differences.

Mrs. Britton's Book Nook. (2019). *Hey, little ant* [Video]. YouTube. https://www.youtube.com/watch?v=ehH6l6v5sYM

This read aloud of the children's book *Hey, Little Ant* by Phillip and Hannah Hoose exposes young listeners to a dilemma—should the ant avoid being trampled?—and a solution.

TED. (2011). *Teaching with the world peace game* [Video]. YouTube. https://www.youtube.com/watch?v=0_UTgoPUTLQ

John Hunter's TED Talk reveals that children are intuitively good negotiators and that in a group they can collectively make valued decisions when they negotiate. To make things more challenging, Hunter assigns one child to act as a saboteur who secretly tries to undermine the others' good efforts.

Other Inquiry Words Starting With N

▸ Negotiated curriculum
▸ Network

‣ Novelty
‣ Nurture

Connections

This chapter is especially related to *D is for Dialogue, J is for Juxtaposing, L is for Listening,* and *R is for Roles.*

Further Reading

Latz, M. (n.d.). *Learning negotiating skills as kids will pay off for a lifetime.* Expert Negotiator. https://www.expertnegotiator.com/tip/learning-negotiating-skills-as-kids

Miller, S. (n.d.). *Ages and stages: Learning to resolve conflicts.* Scholastic. https://www.scholastic.com/teachers/articles/teaching-content/ages-stages-learning-resolve-conflicts

Rowe, M. (n.d.). *The battle for the orange.* Compasito. http://www.eycb.coe.int/compasito/chapter_4/pdf/4_30.pdf

Rowe, M. (n.d.). *The two-dollar game.* https://ocw.mit.edu/courses/sloan-school-of-management/15-667-negotiation-and-conflict-management-spring-2001/lecture-notes/about_game.pdf

O is for Owning

Owning in the inquiry context refers to both investment in and commitment to doing inquiry as an individual or with others, as well as the learner's internalization of inquiry knowledge and strategies. Owning also refers to feeling a strong personal connection to the subject matter or skills that are acquired. Ownership is related to commitment to learning more about the process and content even when not required to do so by the teacher (i.e., saying "this is about me"). Ownership is about empowerment to take the lead in one's learning. It is accompanied by feelings of independence and taking pride in oneself as a learner whether in a particular situation or more generally.

Making Owning Happen

Primary-grade teacher Kate Bodger noted fascinating comments from the students as they worked in their inquiry classroom and then went on a field trip to check their understandings of chickens in an authentic setting (Grow Waitaha, 2017). Kate focused attention on what the students were passionate about. She said,

> I think the one thing that we have noticed is that students are really excited about coming to school because they've got projects that they haven't finished, or something that they want to continue on with, or a work group that they're working with, so the parents are starting to say that their kids are really looking forward to going to school and that they're happy to go to school.

She added that the students were overall more enthusiastic and able to concentrate more.

We made a similar observation in one of the schools we worked with over several years. On one occasion, we arrived at a classroom before the teacher, but the students were already there. Rather than waiting for the teacher to give them instructions about what to do during the upcoming lesson, the students owned the learning situation. They got into work groups and actively engaged in their work before the teacher arrived. They took ownership of the learning tasks and also managed the fair division of effort across the groups, ensuring that everyone was communicating about their goals. A current term for interest-based work centers where students take ownership for their learning is *Makerspaces*.

Barbara Spector and Charles Gibson (1991) studied 572 students' perceptions about what made their learning especially effective in science. Their conclusions can apply across subjects:

> Some of the factors that middle school students perceived as helpful to learning science were (a) experiencing the situations about which they were learning; (b) having live presentations by professional experts; (c) doing hands-on activities; (d) being active learners; (e) using inductive reasoning to generate new knowledge; (f) exploring transdisciplinary approaches to problem solving; (g) having adult mentors; (h) interacting with peers and adults; (i) establishing networks; (j) having close personal friends who shared their interest in learning; (k) trusting

the individuals in their learning environment, including adults and students; and (l) experiencing a sense of self-reliance. (p. 467)

Spector and Gibson incorporated these specific 12 qualities of classroom inquiry that students especially valued within a more complex theoretical model of classroom inquiry. Their model includes a section titled "induction into inquiry"—in other words, making learners members of a community with a sense of ownership over the identity and the process. They suggested that three qualities of teaching and learning especially foster development of this sense of membership and ownership:

> - Solving problems in real world [i.e., authentic] situations.
> - Seeing connections and patterns in own data.
> - Building hypotheses, concepts, & theories grounded in own experiences. (p. 480)

Ownership is greatly aided by actively participating in setting the goals and other planning steps. Making meaningful choices is empowering and part of this process. Students with high self-efficacy are better prepared to take ownership of the process of inquiring and the results of their own and team investigations. In contrast, always waiting for directions from the teacher and striving for high marks or other external forms of approval can be signs of low student ownership of the process and content.

Functioning well with shared ownership in a group or community requires building trust. That trust is created by all members of the classroom together over time and with the help of resources the teacher gathers for students.

Why Owning is Important

Owning is the expression of engagement, confidence, and trust, as well as the knowledge and skill to take responsibility for learning. It is core to collaboration, negotiation, taking initiative, and building lifelong learning dispositions and skills. Owning is an important part of the knowledge, skills, and identity of an inquirer.

See Owning in Action

Edutopia. (2013). *How to get students ready for learning* [Video]. YouTube. https://www.youtube.com/watch?v=-O8t__3Vu9I

A school in Maine uses relationship-building morning meetings and ongoing student-led activities to focus learners and prepare them to learn.

Edutopia. (2019). *Passion-driven research projects* [Video]. YouTube. https://www.youtube.com/watch?v=uHcZlBPD00M

Australian upper elementary students own their own cross-curricular "Enigma Learning" mission: They choose areas they are interested in, write the first 10 questions they want an answer to, write a six-page contract to do research, work on their project, and then present their results to their peers.

Edutopia. (2013). *Reframing failure as iteration allows students to thrive* [Video]. YouTube. https://www.youtube.com/watch?v=qJyNxx82vGQ

A New York City school bases its curriculum around games. Grade 6 students demonstrate ownership of their learning as they build a working Rube Goldberg machine.

Edutopia. (2019). *Sparking curiosity with self-directed learning* [Video]. YouTube. https://www.youtube.com/watch?v=t3vGXmGazJE

An Australian elementary school demonstrates how children own the learning situation by following their interests.

Edutopia. (2015). *Student-led conferences: Empowerment and ownership* [Video]. YouTube. https://www.youtube.com/watch?v=L_WBSInDc2E

In a Chicago, IL, public magnet school, students explain what they are doing in school at parent-teacher conferences.

Edutopia. (2017). *Thinkering studio: Supporting self-directed learning* [Video]. YouTube. https://www.youtube.com/watch?v=Erm2Kokx8R0

Students in grades 5–8 create their own project-based learning activities and identify resources needed for their projects. A general template helps them cover key needs. Teachers ask leading questions and review students' reflective journals.

Grow Waitaha. (2017). *Play-based learning (and inquiry)–supporting learner agency: Part 3* [Video]. YouTube. https://www.youtube.com/watch?v=UV212W8Ln-4

New Zealand grades 3–4 teacher Kate Bodger explains that meaningful dialogue begins by talking with students to find out what interests them. Students then demonstrate learners' ownership of the inquiry process and content, as well as agency and pride in their work. The video also highlights real-world topics, looking for patterns in data, and building concepts based on one's own experiences.

MOE Singapore. (2013). *Learning science through inquiry-based approach* [Video]. YouTube. https://www.youtube.com/watch?v=CWnsxkfoQHo

Singapore students in grades 3 and 4 discuss how they are investigating questions in which they are invested.

Other Inquiry Words Starting With O

- Observing
- Organizing (analyzing and evaluating data or information)
- Originality
- Outcomes

Connections

This chapter is especially related to *A is for Activity, B is for Beginning, C is for Collaborating, G is for Goals, I is for Interests, N is for Negotiating, P is for Process, R is for Roles*, and *V is for Valuing*.

Further Reading

Brejcha, L. (2018). *Makerspaces in school: A month-by-month schoolwide model for building meaningful makerspaces*. Prufrock Press.

Díaz, P. (2020). *A way to promote student voice—literally*. Edutopia. https://www.edutopia.org/article/way-promote-student-voice-literally

Mulvahill, E. (2019). *33 awesome team-building games and activities for kids*. We Are Teachers. https://www.weareteachers.com/team-building-games-and-activities

Renard, L. (2019). *15 fun team building activities and trust games for the classroom*. BookWidgets. https://www.bookwidgets.com/blog/2019/10/15-fun-team-building-activities-and-trust-games-for-the-classroom

Spector, B. S., & Gibson, C. (1991). A qualitative study of middle school students' perceptions of factors facilitating the learning of science: Grounded theory and existing theory. *Journal of Research in Science Teaching, 28*(6), 467–484. https://doi.org/10.1002/tea.3660280603

P is for Process

A process is a deliberate, systematic progression. When it features fixed steps, as in a recipe, it is an algorithm. When it features adaptive, general rules or guidelines, it is a heuristic. The details of the steps are the methodology. Disciplines matter in process: Historians use different methodologies than psychologists, for example.

Making Process Happen

Inquiry as process means using the methodologies of inquiry. Three types of inquiry processes make the most sense for elementary students. Additional details are shared in Table 1. Because inquiry involves heuristic processes (i.e., general guidelines that can be modified to suit the time and circumstances,

Table 1

Summary of Suggested Inquiry Processes

	Topic-Driven Inquiry	Observation-Driven Inquiry	Problem-Solving Inquiry
Grade Levels Best Suited	Lower elementary.	Upper elementary (option 1).	Upper elementary (option 2).
Subjects Best Suited	All, especially social and personal growth.	Especially science and mathematics.	Especially social topics such as local, state, or national issues within students' knowledge range.
Common Methodologies	Simple and guided observations (including basic counts), surveys, and interviews.	Systematic observations and counts, graphs, and charts.	Cases, interviews, photographs, surveys, and summary tables.
Process (Steps)			
Topic Selection	Students select topic with teacher guidance. Topics are commonly general interests.	Teacher identifies about three related topics from recent curriculum. Student teams select one of the topics based on mutual interest. Topics are commonly questions leading to answers or findings.	Teacher usually assigns problem to be discussed and solved. Students work to form a clear problem understanding (representation). Topics are commonly problems leading to solutions.
Review Prior Knowledge	Students (with teacher prompting and leadership as needed) review (access) prior knowledge of the topic (e.g., brainstorming).	Teacher and students together review facts and related ideas learned; a copy of teacher notes on the topic is given to each team.	Students (with teacher prompting and leadership as needed) review prior knowledge, especially review procedures.

Table 1, *continued*

	Topic-Driven Inquiry	Observation-Driven Inquiry	Problem-Solving Inquiry
Organize Knowledge	Students (with teacher prompting and leadership as needed) organize prior knowledge as a group or individually (e.g., semantic/concept map, chart, table).	Students organize prior knowledge in a semantic or concept map with sub-categories (i.e., hierarchical) of the most important topics or ideas, identifying relationships between pairs of concepts (one word or phrase for each connection). Students identify one relationship of most interest and create a researchable question about that relationship (teachers ensure available resources for students to find relevant evidence, or help revise the question).	Students (with teacher prompting and leadership as needed) select available relevant information and separate irrelevant information. Students identify the procedure to solve the problem.
Collect New Data	Students (with teacher prompting and leadership as needed) prepare a map of main ideas from the new information. Link pairs of words, phrases, or ideas based on their experiences. Give reasons for the connections. Write or voice-record report.	Students collect new data as evidence to answer the question (older children can test a hypothesis).	Students collect new information or use given data, follow steps leading to the solution, anticipate if they are leading to a good solution, and write out the solution with explanations.
Share	Students communicate their report to a suitable audience (e.g., classmates, other classes, parents, guests). Teacher puts final reports on display.	Students communicate their report to a suitable audience (e.g., classmates, other classes, parents, guests). Other students rate the believability of findings and give reasons. Teachers puts final reports on display.	Students share solutions with others. Other students might evaluate the solution and procedure.

even within an inquiry sequence), teachers are welcome to adapt the processes to the learning goals, resources, and learners with whom they are working.

Topic-Driven Inquiry

Also called descriptive inquiry, topic-driven inquiry includes reading sources for new information, doing short interviews, or writing simple surveys. We recommend this as the initial inquiry process for primary students. This simple structure for learning about anything of interest demands less prior knowledge, reasoning, and literacy than other inquiry methodologies. Cases present scenarios that apply classroom learning to real-life situations. Usually narratives, these cases can come from students' books, TV, or online. Inquiry should address broad, familiar topics, such as pets, bullying, friendships, or other social experiences. The most effective cases add new information a little at a time, incorporating descriptions and comments. Teachers promote critical thinking by asking students to distinguish facts from assumptions, and to reflect on ways to make their case more authentic by using information from surveys or interviews. For example:

▸ What is the situation?
▸ What problems need solving?
▸ What new information would help? Where can you find that information?
▸ How can you spot similarities and differences in the information?
▸ How will you decide you have found good information?

Question-Driven Inquiry

A well-chosen, higher level question structures the purpose and specifies the topic. Older students have skills and prior knowledge that help them begin to observe systematically, ask specific and high-level questions, consider causality, and use more formal methodology, possibly involving testing hypotheses, reflection, comparing new and prior understanding, and convincing—not just informing—an audience (e.g., knowledge-fair judges).

Topics flow well from previous science or social studies units. Questions should include "Why?" and "How?" but avoid the term *cause-effect* for social phenomena.

Problem-Solving Inquiry

Problem solving has different goals and can take less time. Methodologies differ; for example, students solve arithmetic problems differently from social studies or ecology problems. The teacher chooses the problems to:

▸ build specific knowledge and skills;

▸ kindle interest;

▸ sharpen analytical, planning, and decision-making skills;

▸ develop high-level question-asking and -answering with reasons; and

▸ help students appreciate that problems are not always clear-cut or easily solvable (all the more reason to try!).

Overall Teaching Considerations

Because inquiry is relatively open-ended, it can feel overwhelming for students and teachers. Being enthusiastic, showing humor, and discussing challenges and solutions are useful. Inquiry activities generate considerable buzz among students, so interludes should allow for quiet reading, reflection, and individual pursuits. We also suggest some direct teaching in inquiry and relevant literacy strategies, such as note-taking for data collection, analysis, and reporting project results. Regular, varied, supportive feedback is essential from the teacher, when self-reporting, and from peers.

Why Process is Important

Inquiry processes model experts' thinking. Students learn systematic but flexible ways to explore general curiosities and specific questions, create knowledge comparable to other inquirers', distinguish evidence from opinion or belief, trust their own judgments, and answer the question: How do we know that?

See Process in Action

Crombie, S. (2014). *The benefits of inquiry-based learning* [Video]. YouTube. https://www.youtube.com/watch?v=2ylmVT5lkck

This video is an animated summary of the process skills in inquiry and benefits of inquiry-based learning.

Edutopia. (2014). *Students break the system of bullying in English class* [Video]. YouTube. https://www.youtube.com/watch?v=Ylsh33GrPYE

Children brainstorm an antibullying campaign and, in the course of making their plan, see how all of the concepts they generate are semantically related.

McGraw-Hill PreK–12. (2018). *Carol's classroom: Inquiry* [Video]. YouTube. https://www.youtube.com/watch?v=20c6prOu6mU

Carol outlines the step-by-step process of inquiry in reading and across the curriculum.

Nature video. (2016). *The brain dictionary* [Video]. YouTube. https://www.youtube.com/watch?v=k61nJkx5aDQ

This animation shows how different words activate different parts of the human brain and how words are grouped based on their meaning.

Other Inquiry Words Starting With P

▸ Peer learning
▸ Personal inquiry experience
▸ Planning (for teachers and students)
▸ Problem definition, finding, and solving
▸ Project-based learning
▸ Projects (over an extended period of time, individually or collectively)

Connections

This chapter is especially related to *D is for Dialogue*, *E is for Evidence*, *H is for Hypothesis*, *M is for Meaning*, *Q is for Questions*, *S is for Sharing*, and *Z is for ZPD*.

Further Reading

Brown, A. L. (1992). Design experiments: Theoretical and methodological challenges in creating complex interventions in classroom settings. *Journal of the Learning Sciences, 2*(2), 141–178. https://doi.org/10.1207/s15327809jls0202_2

Brown, A. L. (1994). The advancement of learning. *Educational Researcher, 23*(8), 4–12. https://doi.org/10.3102/0013189X023008004

Quigley, C., Marshall, J. C., Deaton, C. C. M., Cook, M. P., & Padilla, M. (2011). Challenges to inquiry teaching and suggestions for how to meet them. *Science Education, 20*(1), 55–61. https://files.eric.ed.gov/fulltext/EJ9409 39.pdf

Smyth, A., & Miller, C. (2019). *Project-based learning: How to set up rich experiential learning units*. Edutopia. https://www.edutopia.org/article/how-set-rich -experiential-learning-units

Q is for Questions

In a *Parents* magazine interview, Nobel Prize winner Isidor Rabi commented on how he became a scientist (Schulman, 1993). Other Jewish mothers in Brooklyn asked what their children learned in school each day. His mom probed further and asked Rabi if he had asked a good question. Not all students become Nobel-level physicists, not every parent empowers such curiosity, and teachers work with many students. Nonetheless, students' experience with questions in school and at home can change their lives.

Asking questions is fundamental to inquiry. Classroom inquiry ultimately includes students asking questions about things that interest them, sharing responsibility for finding answers, and evaluating all answers. For cultural and personal reasons, or if they were previously rebuffed for asking, some students might hesitate to ask even for clarifications. Teachers need to help learners ask more and better questions, and understand that a good question is sometimes an end in itself. Asking questions that promote inquiry is also a critical teacher function. We address both teacher and student questioning, in turn.

Making Questions Happen

Teacher Questions

Teachers' questions inspire thought and evaluate learning. Questions should vary widely in complexity, guided, for example, by Bloom's revised taxonomy (Anderson & Krathwohl, 2001). Some questions address knowing or understanding. Who, what, when, where, why, and how questions help students remember facts or procedures, but they should be the minority of questions in an inquiry context, particularly if they have been addressed (See *W is for Who, What, When, Where, Why . . . and How*). They can be a good way to start a lesson and connect it to a previous lesson on the same topic. For example, in a primary class, a teacher might ask, "What new words did we learn last Friday? What story did we read about that topic?" In a science class in a higher grade level, a teacher might say, "Let's start with some review before moving on: What does the word *density* mean?" Usually, answers to these lower level questions can be found in the textbook, notes, or online.

Framing higher level questions in the moment is more difficult. It is better to plan several in advance for each class. For example, a question about analyzing nutrition for primary students could be, "How could we tell if a food is sweetened?" After checking for allergies, this question could be explored by having a taste test or having students look at package labels. Learners must relate multiple sources of information. This is important to teach beginning readers, so that they learn how to check their memory of the facts and defend relations they have inferred from the facts. Lesson and unit plans should include several explicit questions, from simple to complex. An advanced social studies analysis, synthesis, and evaluation question could ask students how they think their lives would be different or the same if they lived in a specific different country, and if their lives would be better than now. Before insisting on answers, ask students what they need to know before and how they will find that information.

Student Questions

Students can systematically build skills and dispositions for asking higher level questions in any lesson, activity, or subject. Students can learn the question stems (who, what, when, where, why, and how) and the key terms of Bloom's revised taxonomy (Anderson & Krathwohl, 2001) so that they can evaluate the level of their own questions. Learning to formulate different kinds of questions can be practiced through many activities. Students in pairs or small groups can write one or more questions about a story they read in class or any subject experience. The answers can be the basis of whole-class discussion. A class can have a "What happened?" or "What if?" question board or blog, or take a few minutes of story or topic review before a teacher-led discussion. Students can participate in small-group questioning games, such as "What I think will happen from the story title." The teacher can ask, "How could we use Bill's question to help us learn something interesting?" or "Why is that question important to understanding what happened in our story?" Questions can be encouraged following show-and-tell presentations. Discussions can connect past experiences to new topics or problems. Working in small groups can encourage and cognitively facilitate these capabilities.

To model clear questions and provide a comfort zone for students, pause when asking any question and discuss, "Why do you think I asked that question? How can this question help us learn better or more?" Suggest that students practice wording one kind of question as they read a story silently. Students need frequent reassurance that there is no one correct answer to these questions. Encourage many students to comment, welcome every suggestion with comments such as "Thank you for your interesting thoughts," and schedule pauses in each lesson for students' clarification questions. Mention that other students might appreciate somebody speaking up to ask or answer a question to help explore a story or other lesson.

While creating a plan to teach students kinds of questions or how to question, consider how much class time to devote to this activity. Students of all ages will intuitively begin by asking factual questions that are often worded to favor "yes" or "no" replies. They need modeling and practice asking more open-ended questions, and pursuing answers might occupy hours, days, or weeks.

Finally, give learners time in group or individual projects to reflect back on the process they followed and the questions they asked or recorded to learn about a topic of interest. Posters at science, history, or other knowledge fairs could begin with the question that motivated the presentation as well as a title. At first, we will need to lead students through the steps, but later the students can guide themselves (e.g., What questions captured your interest in this topic?

How did you narrow it down? What other questions could you now ask about this topic? Why are they important?).

Brief reflective discussions after every project are a powerful tool to guide young learners to become aware of their own knowledge about how to self-regulate their future question-asking. This also allows teachers to reward students' accomplishments as part of a community of inquirers.

Why Questions Are Important

Teachers' long-term goal is to create a questioning frame of mind or disposition. The kinds of questions teachers ask are important for inquiry in at least two ways. First, they provide models for students to emulate as they ask questions. Second, they can be used to empower students to pose meaning-seeking questions to themselves, their classmates, and the teacher or other sources of expertise. They accomplish these outcomes, in part, by redefining roles, as Professor Rabi's mother did for him with her query about the good questions he asked at school every day.

Having the efficacy, agency, and skills to ask questions that are acknowledged as meaningful by teachers and fellow students, and that enhance one's own understanding, impacts what happens in the classroom. It continues throughout students' formal education and life as citizens. These skills and dispositions can be learned. Teachers who value inquiry offer students this opportunity by making questions a part of every lesson. What good question have you asked today?

See Questions in Action

Edutopia. (2015). *Inquiry-based learning: Developing student-driven questions* [Video]. YouTube. https://www.youtube.com/watch?v=OdYev6MXTOA

Chicago, IL, magnet school teachers and students from several grades discuss the questions to be pursued within each line of inquiry in the curriculum.

Institute for Inquiry. (n.d.). *Snail investigation*. https://www.exploratorium. edu/education/ifi/inquiry-and-eld/educators-guide/snail-investigation

The text and six videos show how grade 3 students pose questions about snails and follow up with their inquiry.

OESSTA. (2014). *How can I start to plan for inquiry?* [Video]. YouTube. https://www.youtube.com/watch?v=t5TgcuXdCjY

A Canadian teacher and colleagues describe how students created questions and a theme for a unit on freedom. The video also addresses changes in teacher roles, especially regarding facilitating and answering questions.

Rusco, A. (2011). *Bloom's taxonomy feat. Harry Potter.m4v* [Video]. YouTube. https://www.youtube.com/watch?v=TI4kZb0vLiY

Each stage of Bloom's taxonomy is explained, as well as the kinds of questions associated with each, using clips from different *Harry Potter* movies.

TEDx Talks. (2014). *The power of ummm. . . | Kath Murdoch | TEDxWestVancouver ED* [Video]. YouTube. https://www.youtube.com/watch?v=LFt15Ig64Yg

Australian teacher Kath Murdoch's TEDx talk addresses what children are wondering about, using their questions "as a gateway to deep learning." The video stresses the importance of nurturing curiosity in classrooms.

Other Inquiry Words Starting With Q

▸ Quality of evidence
▸ Query
▸ Quizzicality

Connections

This chapter is especially related to *E is for Evidence*, *I is for Interests*, *J is for Juxtaposing*, and *W is for Who, What, When, Where, Why . . . and How.*

Further Reading

Anderson, L. W., & Krathwohl, D. R. (Eds.). (2001). *A taxonomy for learning, teaching, and assessing: A revision of Bloom's taxonomy of educational objectives* (Complete ed.). Longman.
Aulls, M. W. (1978). *Developmental and remedial reading in the middle grades.* Allyn & Bacon.

Delcourt, M. A. B., & McKinnon, J. (2011). Tools for inquiry: Improving questioning in the classroom. *LEARNing Landscapes, 4*(2), 145–159. https://doi.org/10.36510/learnland.v4i2.392

Getzels, J., & Csikszentmihalyi, M. (1976). *The creative vision: A longitudinal study of problem finding in art*. Wiley.

Public Schools of Robeson County. (n.d.). *QAR: Question answer relationship: Teaching children where to seek answers to questions*. https://www.robeson.k12.nc.us/cms/lib/NC01000307/Centricity/Domain/3863/QAR%20Booklet.pdf

Rothstein, D., & Santana, L. (2011). *Make just one change: Teach students to ask their own questions*. Harvard Education Press.

Schulman, M. (1993). Great minds start with questions: Practical ways to enhance your child's natural ability to think and create. *Parents, 68*(9), 99–102.

R is for Roles

A role refers to the nature of the behaviors and responsibilities that individuals take on within a social group. In the classroom, both the teacher and students have roles to fill to set favorable conditions for participants' communication and learning. Classroom social groups differ in size and type, but the word *group* primarily refers to whole-class communication and learning events led by the teacher and subgroups of 2–5 children facilitated by the teacher. In classrooms in which teachers attempt to create an inquiry culture, both teacher and student roles are necessarily more diversified during whole-class or small-group social situations. Attention to roles is an important element in successful approaches to inquiry instruction in the elementary grades.

Making Roles Happen

The words *teacher* and *learner* come from verbs that imply roles. In inquiry classrooms, however, the distinction between these roles is rethought. Both teacher and learner play new, different, and more diverse roles than in traditional classrooms.

While observing several classes in which teachers emphasized inquiry-based instruction, we found a commonality that we later realized was associated with teacher and student roles. In every class, students were actively involved in pairs and small groups, and the teacher was either working with one group or moving among groups—sometimes just observing or acting as a monitor by giving encouragement to a group or pair of students, and sometimes acting in the role of dialogue leader or a coach. No teacher was doing all of the talking with students just listening. The noise level in all of the classes was a tolerable buzzing combined with purposeful student movement.

After several months observing and talking with teachers and students, it became evident that the teachers either explicitly or intuitively assigned students different roles to play during projects and small-group activities. The teachers distributed both academic and social opportunities for students, and responsibilities for the inquiry process. Each of these combinations of activities, opportunities, and responsibilities was a role, and the students all experienced multiple roles.

Roles need to be explained and modeled to clarify role expectations for students during a project. Teachers should discuss:

> ▸ how and why learning will improve if students responsibly take on particular roles,
> ▸ teacher and peer expectations for successfully playing a particular role, and
> ▸ duties and main responsibilities assumed within each role.

Typically, an inquiry project begins with a whole-class, teacher-directed explanation (followed by time-to-time reminders) to students outlining:

> ▸ the type of inquiry process or model to be used,
> ▸ the extent and nature of small-group inquiry activities for the current project, and
> ▸ the introduction and initial practice of student roles in small groups.

In the first month of school, it is helpful to connect the overall system of classroom management to teacher and student roles for inquiry. The system and roles become more stable, at least for the duration of the inquiry unit.

During a year of school, student and teacher inquiry roles are likely to increase in number, and the kinds of roles become more varied. This role diversity happens as a class becomes more experienced doing inquiry projects, and students make a greater commitment to engaging in roles they have used. Many students discover they are more capable than they imagined by taking on new roles as members of an inquiry team.

Over the years of schooling, students and teachers learn to adapt and enact multiple roles. Students become facilitators of each other's learning, and teachers self-check for their own prior knowledge of a subject rather than just moving through a textbook or syllabus. Table 2 highlights a number of student roles that could be performed during different phases of inquiry. Any roles could be added to any of the boxes; these are just examples.

In order to create and sustain a classroom culture in which the teacher and students co-construct the process and content, some important social roles for teachers are advisor, guide, collaborator, friend, and helper. Important academic roles for teachers include leader, modeler of inquiry strategies, facilitator, coach, and curriculum designer. Learners need not necessarily master every role to the same extent, especially if there are preferences or particular talents the student wants to improve.

Why Roles Are Important

Roles are tied to expectations about who says and does what. Roles make collaboration possible. Students have often come to expect that only the teacher has the right to interrupt the person speaking to the whole class. In inquiry classrooms students learn that it is permitted to challenge the teacher and each other with respectful, relevant statements and questions. They also need opportunities to learn new social and academic roles. Multiple and diverse roles are key to inquiry in classrooms.

See Roles in Action

Bri. (2012). *Jigsaw activity* [Video]. YouTube. https://www.youtube.com/watch ?v=D6i7U_99BQY

Jigsaw allows students to enter the role of an expert on a specific topic and then teach what they've learned to their peers. Primary students research animals in this example. The video also illustrates dialogue, monitoring, positive feedback, and active listening.

Table 2

Examples of Student Roles in Different Phases of the Inquiry Process

Inquiry Activity	Whole-Class Roles	Small-Group Roles	Individual Roles
1. Selecting a Topic to Study	• Participant in dialogue	• Participant in pair-share	• Self-checker for prior knowledge
2. Forming a Project Question	• Brainstormer	• Collaborator	• Explainer
3. Clarifying a Project Question (Asking Who, What, Where, Why, When, and How)	• Convergent and divergent question asker, or hypothesizer	• Hypothesizer	• Reasoner • Predicter • Paraphraser
4. Collecting Information	• Brainstormer in planning data collection • Listener • Sharer (of information, dialoguing about possibilities, importance, relevance or source of questionable information)	• Partner • Searcher • Recorder • Help seeker • Memorizer • Checker	• Searcher (for key words or ideas) • Survey giver (and designer of surveys) • Interviewer (and interview question designer) • Reader (to identify general and specific topics, or main ideas) • Observer • Note-taker
5. Analyzing Data (Classifying Concepts and Ideas, Counting Frequencies, Explaining Findings)	• Reasoner • Argument generator	• Analyst • Tutor • Help seeker • Monitor • Dialoguer • Summarizer	• Explainer • Checker
6. Presenting Inquiry Report or Presentation (Written Reports, Slide Show, Graph or Chart, Oral Report)	• Listener	• Audience member • Question asker • Speaker • Manager of audience participation	• Author • Paragraph writer • Summary writer • Report writer

Core Education. (2010). *Changing roles of teachers and learners* [Video]. YouTube. https://www.youtube.com/watch?v=nuYWUPirkqQ

A New Zealand educator describes the changing roles of teachers and learners. A challenge is to encourage student creativity in a system originally designed to create conformity. His favorite term for the teacher is "experienced learner."

Crombie, S. (2014). *Teacher's role in inquiry-based learning* [Video]. YouTube. https://www.youtube.com/watch?v=mdVWb27z0Zc

This animated summary of the teacher's role in inquiry-based teaching also touches upon scaffolding and facilitating questioning. Teachers' effectiveness increases as they gradually give students control and time to answer questions.

Debroy, A. (2018). *5 best videos to refer for classroom strategies for inquiry based learning.* EdTechReview. https://edtechreview.in/trends-insights/insights/3337-5-best-videos-to-refer-for-classroom-strategies-for-inquiry-based-learning

Actual classrooms are shown in this series of videos connected by text. The third video particularly focuses on changing teacher roles, especially being a facilitator.

Edmonton Regional Learning Consortium – ERLC. (2016). *Inquiry in social studies* [Video]. YouTube. https://www.youtube.com/watch?v=goln0EntxYM

Two Edmonton, Alberta, teachers discuss the outcomes of elementary school inquiry involvement, including curriculum content, deep engagement, changing roles, facilitating, and learning along with the students.

Edmonton Regional Learning Consortium – ERLC. (2016). *Inquiry in social studies - Kelsey's story* [Video]. YouTube. https://www.youtube.com/watch?v=1JVOFrCORQ4

An Edmonton, Alberta, teacher describes how inquiry has changed her role in the classroom.

Other Inquiry Words Starting With R

▸ Real-world experiences
▸ Reflecting and reflection

- ‣ Relationships
- ‣ Relinquish control
- ‣ Representing results (see *P is for Process* and *S is for Sharing*)
- ‣ Responsibility (see *O is for Owning*)
- ‣ Results (similar to outcomes; see *P is for Process*)

Connections

This chapter is especially related to *A is for Activity*, *C is for Collaborating*, and *S is for Sharing*.

Further Reading

Aulls, M. W., & Ibrahim, A. (2012). Pre-service teachers' perceptions of effective inquiry instruction: Are effective instruction and effective inquiry instruction essentially the same? *Instructional Science, 40*(1), 119–139. https://doi.org/10.1007/s11251-010-9164-z

Walker, C. L., & Shore, B. M. (2015). Understanding classroom roles in inquiry education: Linking role theory and social constructivism to the concept of role diversification. *SAGE Open, 5*(4), 1–13. https://doi.org/10.1177/2158244015607584

Walker, C. L., Shore, B. M., & Tabatabai, D. (2013). Eye of the beholder: Investigating the interplay between inquiry role diversification and social perspective taking. *International Journal of Educational Psychology, 2*(2), 144–192. https://doi.org/10.4471/ijep.2013.23

S is for Sharing

Sharing happens all of the time in an inquiry-based classroom. Sharing requires having something to share, so this chapter focuses on collecting data as an important context for sharing among students. Sharing has a communication component and a distribution component. During collaborative data collection, students divide up the search for information but communicate with their group what they are finding, disclose possible sources that others may also find relevant, help each other organize the resulting facts and concepts, and make decisions about what data are most important and what information is confusing or irrelevant. Through sharing, the whole becomes more than the sum of the parts.

Making Sharing Happen

In primary grades, students who can write their own name and copy words, or produce phonetic versions of words, can also collect data. They become more aware of the value of sharing as inquirers working together. At first, inquiry and sharing depend on teacher-class dialogue. An inquiry experience can be based on reading a book aloud to engage students in predicting, clarifying words, and clarifying relationships between the information in pictures. The teacher can model "I wonder" statements and invite students to pose these questions. The teacher can model summarizing what was said or what happened before, predicting how the book will evolve. Students can be invited to help summarize or identify main topics. All of the literacy, thinking, listening, and collaborating strategies are relevant to sharing, and especially data collection, within inquiry. Through such regular inquiry-based oral reading sessions, students learn and use the language of inquiring (e.g., "Yes, Billy, your prediction about what would happen next actually happened!").

Observing and asking questions together is sharing. For example, inquiry might begin with 2 weeks of learning to care for a pair of turtles. Predictions about what and how to feed and handle the turtles can be confirmed or disconfirmed after a few days of observing and caring for them. Seeking evidence to confirm or disconfirm is data collection. Questions are important while collecting information. For example, in an actual classroom experience like this, the teacher and students ask questions such as, "How do you know if a turtle is asleep or awake?"

A more systematic means of collecting data could be having pairs of student investigators take photographs of the turtles at different times and write simple lists. Sharing can be extended to keeping a class notebook or log. Comparing data across days can answer the inquiry question: What different things do turtles do during the school day? This project research question arises from the data rather than being set in advance. This also occurs in case studies done by professional researchers whose goal is to describe events in order to gain a deeper understanding of a phenomenon.

One common lower elementary grade activity to promote sharing is to have each student lie down on a section of brown paper as long as their body. The teacher outlines the body, and then asks each student for descriptions of their hair color, etc., and guides them to draw in details. The questions all address: What do I look like? First and second graders and the teacher can then discuss data as the words or facts that help describe people, animals, objects, places, or activities.

At upper elementary grades, a related activity is to pair children who spend time together most days and ask them to choose an activity they do together, such as jumping rope, drawing pictures, lining up for lunch, taking pictures of each other. Ask them to draw a picture of themselves together doing the activity and then to write down words that describe the people, objects, and actions in their picture. The teacher can have the same conversation about what data are. With older children, students can share their list of words with another pair or the class, and then give them three chances to guess the shared activity. These and many other activities (e.g., show and tell) enable dialogue about why people collect and share information and what students can learn from the process.

In intermediate grades, collecting data becomes more sophisticated. For example, collecting information through interviews is always exciting. Moreover, it brings up important process issues, such as, "Should we ask only specific questions or broader questions?" and "Should we prompt the interviewees to say more, clarify, or relate their answer to something they said earlier in the interview?" Before interviewing, the class must establish a topic and write questions they want the interviewee to inform them about. Students must also consider whom to interview, such as other students, teachers, the school head, parents, relatives, athletes, professors, community professionals, or members of city council, congress, or parliament. Learning to write different kinds of questions becomes an authentic and challenging part of collecting data. Students can also collect data by watching relevant videos and asking questions to identify main points, topics, and subtopics.

Many opportunities to share arise during the process of collecting data to learn more about an interesting topic or to test a research question. These opportunities occur while asking questions, observing, comparing and contrasting data, reading different sources to identify details, topics, or main ideas, recording, and organizing information. Several reading and writing strategies can be integrated with the curriculum and practiced during data collection, such as:

- writing notes, lists, reminders, reflections, memos on new ideas, questions and answers, and summaries of notes or readings;
- comparing what is alike and different from multiple sources on the same topic or question;
- interpreting by paraphrasing sentences;
- categorizing topics in notes into common groups of concepts or ideas;
- generating main ideas;
- making a claim and offering evidence to support or refute it; and
- communicating data collection results.

Why Sharing is Important

Inquiry as a process could not be done without sharing and collecting data. The modern world is too complex for anyone acting alone to solve major problems, although every contribution, like votes, adds up. Systematically and collaboratively collecting information depends upon several academic and social skills. We have emphasized many of the academic skills previously. The social skills and dispositions include generosity of spirit, integrity, and trust to share. These, too, can be well learned at school, especially through frequent, varied, and extended involvement in inquiry.

See Sharing in Action

KSmithSchool. (2013). *6th grade project presentation: Design a restaurant for your community* [Video]. YouTube. https://www.youtube.com/watch?v=ekHPTO_5ry4

A California classroom presents its concept for a space-themed restaurant.

Ianimatestuff. (2012). *Best 3rd grade speech ever!!!* [Video]. YouTube. https://www.youtube.com/watch?v=oWCrSxjppaA

A grade 3 student gives his prize-winning speech about personal heroes to his school assembly.

Reading Rockets. (2014). *Students take charge: Reciprocal teaching* [Video]. YouTube. https://www.youtube.com/watch?v=My68SDGeTHI

A Washington state teacher and students demonstrate how to initiate and sustain reciprocal teaching as part of a reading program.

SanBdoCitySchools. (2019). *Using reciprocal teaching to engage 3rd grade readers* [Video]. YouTube. https://www.youtube.com/watch?v=tC032EkLC3A

Grade 3 teacher Carol Sole engages her students in demonstrating reciprocal teaching as students take on several new roles.

Other Inquiry Words Starting With S

▸ Safety (with equipment or materials; while sharing unusual ideas)
▸ Searching
▸ Self-directed learning through projects
▸ Self-efficacy
▸ Self-monitoring
▸ Self-regulated or self-regulating learning (not the same as self-regulation)
▸ Strategies
▸ Student-centered

Connections

This chapter is especially related to *C is for Collaborating, D is for Dialogue, G is for Goals, I is for Interests, L is for Listening, O is for Owning,* and *V is for Valuing.*

Further Reading

Bell, C. V. (2013). Uptake as a mechanism to promote student learning. *International Journal of Education in Mathematics, Science and Technology, 1*(4), 217–229. https://files.eric.ed.gov/fulltext/ED548246.pdf

Costas, E. F. (1996). *Teaching interviewing skills to elementary students* (ED399583). ERIC. https://files.eric.ed.gov/fulltext/ED399583.pdf

Crawford, C. (2018). *How to interview your family.* Scholastic. https://www.scholastic.com/teachers/blog-posts/christy-crawford/valuing-your-history

The Critical Thinking Consortium. (n.d.). *Interviewing techniques.* https://tc2.ca/uploads/PDFs/T4T%20Samples/Interviewing_techniques.pdf

Farrell, S. (2016). *Open-ended vs. closed-ended questions in user research.* Nielsen Norman Group. https://www.nngroup.com/articles/open-ended-questions

Juskow, B. (2005). *Speakers' club: Public speaking for young people.* Prufrock Press.

Palincsar, A. S., & Brown, A. L. (1984). Reciprocal teaching of comprehension-fostering and comprehension-monitoring activities. *Cognition and Instruction, 1*(2), 117–175. https://doi.org/10.1207/s1532690xci0102_1

Reed, P. (2016). *Reciprocal math teaching.* https://www.corelaboratewa.org/blog/teacher-leaders/single/~board/teacher-leaders-archive/post/reciprocal-math-teaching

Thomas, J. W. (2000). *A review of research on project-based learning.* Autodesk.

T is for Talk Time

Two important considerations about talk time include (a) the total amount of time in classes during which anyone is talking, and (b) who is talking and with whom? Teachers talk to the class, groups, or individual students. Students talk to the teacher, answering questions, seeking clarification, or asking for some kind of permission. Finally, students talk with each other, and this dialogue is critical to inquiry-based learning and to the creation of understanding or meaning. Talk time is the measure of the quantity of any of these.

Making Talk Time Happen

There is always a lot of talk in an inquiry class. We suggest aiming for less teacher talk time—as low as 30% of the total—compared to student talk time.

We also propose that more of the student talk time should be dialogue between and among students, not between students and the teacher. In a grade 4 inquiry class we observed, students told us that the teacher had a general rule: "Ask two other students before you ask me." The students loved that idea. It helped them value and support their ownership of the learning. It made them feel proud.

In another example, a teacher of middle school French assigned students to choose a personal hero they admired and then introduce that person to the class through a combination of oral presentation, pictures, artifacts, or other ways that they could creatively devise—all in their second language. One girl, dressed in her self-designed period costume, shared why she admired Laura Secord. Secord was a Canadian hero who ran through the forest during the War of 1812 to warn the British garrison that the Americans were attempting an invasion of the Niagara escarpment. A boy in the same class, who greatly admired a hockey player, talked about the player, displayed his uniform sweater, and invited the player to the class. His hero was his uncle.

Several inquiry words in this book contain ideas for ways to vary the talk patterns used during inquiry classes (see *D is for Dialogue*, *L is for Listening*, *Q is for Questions*, and *R is for Roles*). These include planning time for student-student dialogue in every lesson; explicitly teaching students to ask, answer, and evaluate high-level questions; and looking for different ways for students to teach their fellow students through research presentations, group activities, brainstorming, and sharing experiences. Quiet time for working individually to solve problems or collectively to carry out projects is an additional way to reduce teacher talk time.

Why Talk Time is Important

Of course, students learn from listening to teachers, and there is always a place for some direct teaching. But learning is in general more personally meaningful when students actively own it. Vygotsky's (1978) social constructivist theory shows that student-student dialogue appears to be among the most powerful tools for creating deep understanding. That is why teachers need to talk less in class and create more situations in which students successfully engage verbally with each other.

See Talk Time in Action

Aflatoun International. (2016). *Aflatoun active learning methods: Teacher talking time vs student talking time* [Video]. YouTube. https://www.youtube.com/watch?v=SiL1rtjOCpY

This animation from The Netherlands presents multiple tips to increase student versus teacher talk time: for example, elicit rather than tell, remove yourself from the conversation, and use techniques such as Think-Pair-Share.

DePaul Teaching Commons. (2013). *If I knew then, what I know now: Teacher talk vs. student talk* [Video]. YouTube. https://www.youtube.com/watch?v=ckn2mdb0L5U

The speaker, a drama teacher, talks about how a professor observed his student teaching and recorded TT (teacher talk) or ST (student talk) in his class every minute during a one-hour period. During the debriefing in her office, the professor noted that the ratio of TT:ST was 80:20 and that he was talking too much. But, she said, as a young teacher, he was not alone. He gradually changed that ratio.

Edutopia. (2016). *Oracy in the classroom: Strategies for effective talk* [Video]. YouTube. https://www.youtube.com/watch?v=2ADAY9AQm54

Children in a London, England, school engage in animated discussion about why families have come from other countries. Students talk considerably more than the teacher.

Scholastic. (2017). *Ten tips with Kylene Beers & Robert E. Probst: Tip 1 teach more by talking less* [Video]. YouTube. https://www.youtube.com/watch?v=OD2A9mD1RNE

The two hosts propose open-ended teacher questions rather than ones with specific answers, having children work in pairs, and staying alert to who is talking in the classroom.

Other Inquiry Words Starting With T

- Taking ownership
- Task
- Task commitment

- ▸ Testing hypotheses
- ▸ Theme
- ▸ Treat everyone's opinion as important

Connections

This chapter is especially related to *D is for Dialogue, F is for Facilitating, L is for Listening, M is for Meaning, Q is for Questions, R is for Roles, W is for Who, What, When, Where, Why . . . and How*, and *Z is for ZPD*.

Further Reading

Barkley, S. (2018). *Teacher talk and student talk*. https://barkleypd.com/blog/teacher-talk-student-talk

Filler, T. (2017). *Limiting "teacher talk," increasing student work!* Achieve the Core. https://achievethecore.org/aligned/limiting-teacher-talk-increasing-student-work

Vygotsky, L. S. (1978). *Mind in society* (Trans. M. Cole). Harvard University Press.

U is for Uncertainty

Uncertainty is not having complete, certain knowledge about something. Uncertainty can be a driving force to inquire because students want to know more about something, and it can also be the outcome when they uncover more questions with their answers. Uncertainty has an emotional or motivational side; uncertainty should be at an optimal level that spurs action but does not become debilitating. This boundary varies among individuals, so teachers must try to create an intellectually and emotionally comfortable zone around uncertainty.

Making Uncertainty Happen

Making uncertainty happen requires comfort with the reality that people are not and cannot be certain of everything. Philosopher Imre Lakatos (1976) imagined a dialogue between two mathematicians. One said,

> Really, Lambda, your unquenchable thirst for certainty is becoming tiresome! How many times do I have to tell you that we know nothing for certain? But your desire for certainty is making you raise very boring problems—and is blinding you to the interesting ones. (p. 134)

Members of classrooms should explore things that interest them, ask what they know and what they would want to learn, and make the unknown non-threatening. This reassures students who fear the unknown that others also have gaps in their knowledge that they can openly acknowledge. When reviewing existing knowledge, as when beginning a new curriculum unit, teachers can also ask students to suggest what they do not yet know but might be curious about. Positive teachers' responses build students' confidence that their worth does not depend solely on correct answers. When teachers share that they have uncertainties, they model what they teach. It is acceptable to answer a student's questions with, "I'm not sure; how can we find out?"

In language arts, literature, and social sciences, learners enjoy being read to. This provides opportunities for the teacher to pause and ask where the narrative leads (e.g., "Are we sure? Might different options make sense? Do some questions have several good answers? Or none at all?"). Some books, biographies, or news reports introduce especially rich vocabulary (e.g., "Are we certain what these words mean?"). Modeling use of dictionaries and thesauruses also reinforces comfort with uncertainty. With older students, current events are still unfolding, and sometimes history gets reinterpreted. Have students inquire into different interpretations, find evidence that supports and refutes each interpretation, and decide what they might do next if they do not get an immediate, convincing answer.

Uncertainty is also an important part of writing a story, composition, letter, or a happy-birthday email to a friend. Writers start with an incomplete idea of what words will come out. Students can reduce uncertainty by planning, such as outlining before they start writing and revising until they or the teacher are pleased. The same is true for sculpting with clay, drawing a picture, composing a melody, or arranging a tune or song they already know. Every creative act begins with some uncertainty. Students can reduce the uncertainty by planning, sketching, revising, and sometimes taking a break and doing something else.

In arithmetic, with older elementary students, introduce uncertainties while playing with number ideas: For example, is it always certain that 2 + 5 = 7? Suppose you only had the numbers from 0 to 5 instead of 0 to 9. Would the *idea* of "six" still be true? If you have only 10 numbers from 0 to 9, how do you *write* the number that is one more than 9? How could you write the number that expresses the idea "six" if you only had the numbers 0 to 5? Is it also possible that 2 + 5 = 11? (*Note.* 2 + 5 does equal 11 in "base 6" arithmetic, which is a way to introduce the idea of base.)

Science and technology are also filled with uncertainties: For example, how do you solve the problem of plastic waste in the ocean? Can you stop sea-level rise before you need submarines to visit New York or Venice or Sydney? How can you feed 7 billion people? If you're not sure, how can you find out more? In science, students do a lot of measuring, and it is possible to make unintentional small errors in measurement. That is why scientists make multiple measurements and use the average as the best estimate. When scientists use better measuring devices, such as digital thermometers or laser measuring tools, they reduce the uncertainty, but it never goes away completely.

Uncertainty is not a weakness. That is why there are maps and GPS to guide drivers, and tourist offices and travel agencies to help people plan trips. Uncertainty should trigger exploration and searches for good ideas, not scare students into avoiding questions that do not have straightforward answers. Dealing with uncertainty helps students distinguish among beliefs, assumptions, hypotheses, and knowledge. If we are honest about what we do not fully know and show that the "truth" is sometimes hard to nail down, then our students can also learn to express similar honesty and comfort with uncertainty.

Why Uncertainty is Important

Recognizing uncertainty is a springboard for inquiry and creativity. It helps students listen better and value other's contributions. For almost a century, the Heisenberg uncertainty principle has guided physics and influenced popular culture. It states that one cannot simultaneously know the exact position and the velocity of any object. The more precisely a person knows one thing, the less they can know the other. In short, the universe is filled with both certainties and uncertainties. Teachers and students need to accept uncertainty and make it work for them.

See Uncertainty in Action

NGS Navigators (Producer). (2019, March 7). *Productive uncertainty in elementary science with Dr. Eve Manz* (No. 21) [Audio podcast episode]. https://www.ngsnavigators.com/blog/021

Scientific uncertainty is the springboard for intellectual challenges and advancing knowledge. This podcast episode discusses how to engage uncertainty in teaching, support student discourse through uncertainty and disagreement, and involve students in scientific uncertainty.

Physics Online. (2015). *A level practical endorsement – percentage uncertainty for multiple readings* [Video]. YouTube. https://www.youtube.com/watch?v=YImQNPK3dK0

Use of a digital caliper to measure the diameter of a round toy demonstrates that even apparently precise measurements vary slightly upon repetition. The exact value is uncertain. Accuracy of the estimate is increased by taking multiple measurements and averaging them. The video introduces the concept of the Percentage Uncertainty = Half the Range of the Measures divided by the Average or Mean Measure. Why half? Half of the uncertainty is above the mean, and half below, so this avoids overestimating the uncertainty.

TED-Ed. (2014). *What is the Heisenberg uncertainty principle? – Chad Orzel* [Video]. YouTube. https://www.youtube.com/watch?v=TQKELOE9eY4

This TED-Ed animation explains the quantum physics principle that has found its way into common speech. For any particle that moves (e.g., an electron), it is impossible to know its velocity and position at the same time. A person can know where a particle is, or how quickly it is moving, but cannot know both. In many circumstances, students cannot be certain about every relevant characteristic and must live with a degree of uncertainty.

Villa, S. A. (2016). *Parallax error (how parallax error happens, how to avoid parallax error)* [Video]. YouTube. https://www.youtube.com/watch?v=jr50cmfR61o

This illustrated video shows how eye position can lead to uncertainty in the accuracy of measurements read from instruments.

Other Inquiry Words Starting With U

- ▸ Unbounded (limitless curriculum opportunities)
- ▸ Understanding (see *M is for Meaning*)
- ▸ Undertaking projects
- ▸ Unfazed (difficulties are normal)

Connections

This chapter is especially related to *E is for Evidence*, *H is for Hypothesis*, *L is for Listening*, *P is for Process*, and *Q is for Questions*.

Further Reading

Barron, F. (1958). The psychology of imagination. *Scientific American, 199*(3), 150–166.

Gabella, M. S. (1995). Unlearning uncertainty: Toward a culture of student inquiry. *Theory into Practice, 34*(4), 236–242.

Kostelyk, S. (n.d.). *10 children's books with surprise endings.* https://www.the chaosandtheclutter.com/archives/10-childrens-books-with-surprise-end ings

Lakatos, I. (1976). *Proofs and refutations: The logic of mathematical discovery.* Cambridge University Press.

V is for Valuing

Valuing in absolute terms means evaluating the importance of something alone (e.g., a good reputation, new skills, a comfortable armchair, a friendship). Valuing in relative terms involves juxtaposing alternatives (e.g., working alone versus with a group, whistleblowing or staying uncomfortable while keeping silent, studying history or mathematics, choosing peas versus carrots with a meal). Valuing involves judgments about oneself, others, objects, ideas, goals, curriculum, evidence, and more. It is part of evaluating, which is one of the highest levels in Bloom's revised taxonomy of educational objectives (Anderson & Krathwohl, 2001). It is inherent in every choice students make, and therefore an important part of inquiry.

Making Valuing Happen

Four students in grades 4 and 5 worked together with LEGO materials in a science and computer class to build a machine that demonstrated the principle of mechanical advantage (using gears, levers, or pulleys to reduce the effort required to move a heavier object, but doing so less quickly, as when selecting a lower gear on a bicycle or car). We visited the classroom to watch them work, looking especially at how disagreements, at any stage of their inquiry process, got resolved. Sometimes the teacher intervened, but learner dialogue resolved the following task (Barfurth & Shore, 2008):

Patricia:	You know what we could do, we could put a big gear here like another big gear.
Kenny:	No, it will slow it down.
Filene:	We don't have any big gears.
Kenny:	Plus we don't have it. Plus it will ooh.
Patricia:	We could put the small one attached here *(points to first axle large gear)* and here *(looks like the second axle medium gear)*.
Kenny:	*(Playing with black LEGO chain)* But the big gear, if we put a big gear it will go much slower cause the big gear ahh is much slower. If we add a big gear here *(points to third axle area)* it won't go as fast, Filene. Believe me.
Filene:	Oh, because this one *(nods her head)*. I get it.
Kenny:	No, because the big gears are slower. Some girls are just//
Patricia:	*(Sliding a fourth axle onto the invention with the small gear on the inside)* No *(to Kenny)*, but this one *(points to small gear)* attached to the big gear will go even faster. (p. 153)

This exchange featured students accepting disagreement as a valuable part of normal problem-solving interaction. However, Kenny undervalued girls' contributions—a teachable moment. In the course of another group's discourse, one child alerted the group that everyone should pause to value a suggestion by a student whom the group was ignoring.

The study that featured these interactions (Barfurth & Shore, 2008) identified other verbal interactions that represent engagement in valued means to navigate disagreement among students during inquiry. Useful "moves" that students could bring to disagreements include: (a) maintaining their position (not necessarily implying stubbornness, but rather confidence in one's own understanding—in turn, this confidence engenders courtesy and respect); (b) introducing information; (c) integrating another's position; (d) requesting explanation; (e) modifying one's position; or (f) as also happened, encouraging the group to listen to a good idea from someone who is quiet or being ignored.

Another study revealed values about common practice in inquiry classrooms (Saunders-Stewart et al., 2013). Teachers and parents of gifted students were asked to rate how importantly they regarded classroom group work. Teachers rated it higher. Parents perhaps regarded the situation competitively or were concerned about diluted attention to their students. This example shows how valuing impacts classroom inquiry and differs among groups. For teachers, valuing can involve choosing what it means to "cover" prescribed content, trusting learners to do complex tasks or ask important questions, and communicating openly with parents about why they do inquiry. Parents need to trust that teachers value their students' strengths and needs, and that teachers structure collaboration positively. Therefore, teachers must actively monitor group activities, circulate among groups, listen to how the students interact with each other, and promote positive skills.

Valuing appears in inquiry in many ways. Here are some ideas for how we can build students' ability to be aware of and engage in valuing:

▸ **Valuing knowledge and learning:** Be enthusiastic about our own and students' new learning. Do not condone poking fun at knowledge or knowledgeable people. Stereotypes such as "nerd" should, with kindness, be discussed and dispelled.

▸ **Valuing other learners' opinions:** Active listening, turn-taking, acknowledging and thanking prior contributors, summarizing other's contributions, and games, such as passing a message down a line of people, can help. These strategies can be explored in small skits the students write, improvise, or perform (e.g., with puppets) to overcome shyness.

▸ **Valuing one's own judgment:** By secondary school, students often have more confidence in what a teacher, textbook, or other source tells them than in their own thinking. Inquiry-oriented teachers sometimes greatly diminish the use of textbooks, and frequently reassure learners that they can, alone or with others, create valuable questions and conclusions.

▸ **Valuing collaboration:** Students learn better and learn more when assisted by dialogue. To gain this assurance, students need to frequently experience such interaction. Plan regularly for student-student interaction in every lesson and at every stage of a teaching unit (e.g., planning, enacting, and reflection afterward).

Why Valuing is Important

Students should be aware of the values they assign to what they do, their own needs as well as the needs and contributions of others, and how their needs compare to those of others. This awareness goes far beyond classroom learning. It impacts the choices of the people they want to be with, their careers, and their hobbies; how they define and model good citizenship and social responsibility; and how they are listened to and valued in return. Openly addressing valuing during inquiry helps learners keep their values explicit and stay open to new information or outreach from others who can teach them something interesting, or even make them better people.

See Valuing in Action

Pinkston, C. (2016). *Teaching children philosophy, or how 8-year-olds agree to disagree*. University of Oregon. https://around.uoregon.edu/content/teaching-children-philosophy-or-how-8-year-olds-agree-disagree

In this article and accompanying video, children share opinions about real-world topics such as lying, fair share, and friendship while respecting and learning from others with whom they disagree.

RRFTS. (2014) *JoanAndNathanTalk 5001* [Video]. YouTube. https://www.youtube.com/watch?v=EMgZHeZTeFc

Teacher Joan chats with young Nathan during lunch. She listens attentively, reflects, paraphrases, encourages, probes, and gives supportive feedback. His sense of agency and being valued support his engagement and expressiveness.

Sami, O. (2019). *Sam and the plant next door* [Film]. Whatnot Film. https://aeon.co/videos/to-fight-a-nearby-nuclear-plant-11-year-old-sam-must-win-his-own-ethical-battle

The plant is a new nuclear electricity-generating station. In this short documentary, Sam struggles to reconcile his values regarding the environment with the realities he observes next door. Many candid conversations are shown among friends.

Other Inquiry Words Starting With V

- Variability (contributes to uncertainty; see *U is for Uncertainty*)
- Variety (many ways to implement inquiry-based instruction)
- Verifying (see *E is for Evidence*)
- Vocabulary appropriate to the audience and topic (see *S is for Sharing*)
- Vygotsky, Lev (see *Z is for ZPD*)

Connections

This chapter is especially related to *D is for Dialogue*, *E is for Evidence*, *G is for Goals*, *L is for Listening*, *S is for Sharing*, and *U is for Uncertainty*.

Further Reading

Anderson, L. W., & Krathwohl, D. R. (Eds.). (2001). *A taxonomy for learning, teaching, and assessing: A revision of Bloom's taxonomy of educational objectives* (Complete ed.). Longman.

Barfurth, M. A., & Shore, B. M. (2008). White water during inquiry learning: Understanding the place of disagreements in the process of collaboration. In B. M. Shore, M. W. Aulls, & M. A. B. Delcourt (Eds.), *Inquiry in education: Overcoming barriers to successful implementation* (Vol. 2, pp. 149–164). Routledge.

Gabella, M. S. (1994). Beyond the looking glass: Bringing students into the conversation of historical inquiry. *Theory and Research in Social Education, 22*(3), 340–363. https://doi.org/10.1080/00933104.1994.10505728

Saunders-Stewart, K. S., Walker, C. L., & Shore, B. M. (2013). How do parents and teachers of gifted students perceive group work in classrooms? *Gifted and Talented International, 28*(1–2), 99–106. https://doi.org/10.1080/15332276.2013.11678406

W is for Who, What, When, Where, Why . . . and How

The five W plus H questions represent the reporter's or storyteller's basic questions. *Who*, *where*, and *when* are essentially factual words. *Why* and *how* involve more critical thinking. *What* can be either, depending on its use. The five question stems starting with W, in particular, represent a specific case of eliciting thinking and responses to a printed text, notably news-oriented texts. The questions are important enough to stand alone, especially as a starting point for younger students to gather data that describe a phenomenon. These words act as devices to help unpack the facts any text reveals.

Making Who, What, When, Where, Why . . . and How Happen

Inquiry starts with wanting to learn more. A common first step is acquiring new facts that build new understandings. Acquisition of factual information includes reading in such ways that facts can be recalled, used, and discussed. These question stems can easily be taught to students, who can then use the questions while quizzing themselves or others.

While reading to collect new information, answers to factual questions— *who*, *where*, *when*, and often *what*—are found in the statements within the materials. In contrast, answers to critical thinking questions—*why*, *how*, and sometimes *what*—require the reader to interrelate statements in the text and with prior knowledge. When answering "What happened?" the *what* is about facts. But sometimes a question asks, "What is the difference between this and that? What would happen if this occurred? What is like this?" Like *how* and *why*, these *what* questions invoke critical thinking. All learners benefit from understanding this distinction.

Getting, remembering, and interrelating facts, and being sensitive to missing facts, facilitate the larger goals of learning how to inquire alone or together and writing about the facts. Primary grade teachers can profitably teach, guide, and practice using the question stems. Upper grade teachers can also practice while introducing note-taking and summarizing to further help students selectively collect information and shape it into results that can be written and presented to suitable audiences. Practice activities, with questions based on readings in a story, news report, or paragraphs of informative resources, might include the following:

- ▸ the teacher or classmates ask different questions using the question stems to extract the facts stated in the text itself and in students' answers to such questions;
- ▸ while reading, students use the question stems as categories to record facts as notes about main topics and phrases to be recalled later;
- ▸ after reading, students reduce many facts to a few that capture the key message in what was read; or
- ▸ the class discusses notes based on the question stems with classmates to identify the most important information.

Teachers can also guide students to check if important facts on a topic might be missing. Imagine a group project on ancient Egypt's great pyramids. One student reads a sentence, such as, "Ancient Egyptians were impressive engineers because they built giant pyramids as tall as 480 feet, practically by hand." The student wants to share the information by asking questions to see if group members consider it new and interesting: "Who built the pyramids? What is their height? Where are they?" Students can read these facts in the written sentence. However, the sentence does not state precisely *when* or *where* the pyramids were built. It gives just a snippet about *how* or with *what* material, and nothing about *why*. The alert inquirer might use the set of questions to infer what potentially valuable information is missing and requires further data collection.

In addition to focusing on the critical skills of reading and writing, the question stems can be reinforced with simple songs and games. Students can take turns asking each other a series of questions about an event, a show-and-tell object, or a story read by the teacher. Older students can investigate news and other information that interest them, and apply the question stems to original compositions. Then they can go on to ask questions about connections and what they do not yet know.

Teachers might apply the question stems to a *Dora the Explorer* video or an old Sherlock Holmes movie. Students can watch for how and when the collaborators ask *who*, *what*, *when*, *where*, *why*, and *how*, or other questions. Older students can follow the investigators in Nancy Drew and Hardy Boys adventure novels, as well as some of the less violent Agatha Christie books featuring analytical Belgian police Inspector Hercule Poirot. Yes, these are old tales, but they have relatively simple storylines and are widely available. All are good to read to the students in story time—with some note-taking and discussion.

Why Who, What, When, Where, Why . . . and How Are Important

The *who*, *what*, *when*, *where*, *why*, and *how* questions are easy-to-learn starting points for supporting literacy development, giving students both skills and agency to ask and answer questions, and helping them systematically attend to, evaluate, and organize new data on a topic while they obtain information. These inquiry questions support remembering, reflecting, and sharing facts and understanding with an inquiry team. They are helpful to keep on hand for use in a later presentation or descriptive report, and sometimes after a presentation to test what the audience remembers. The question stems can lead directly to related skills in making displays, information tables, timelines, charts, graphs, and other communication tools. They fit well with independent reading and stories or factual material read by the teacher.

See Who, What, When, Where, Why . . . and How in Action

ESL Games Plus. (n.d.). *Question words—What, where, who, why, when, which, how, grammar activity* [Video game]. https://www.eslgamesplus.com/question-words-what-where-who-why-when-which-how-grammar-activity

This promotion for early readers' literacy games includes a *Sentence Monkey* sample in which the student drags and drops the appropriate question word into the oval for the missing word in a sentence, and then clicks on "submit" to check the answer. The game could be played in pairs or small groups.

Jack Hartmann Kids Music Channel. (2016). *6 questions | Fun reading & writing comprehension strategy for kids | Jack Hartmann* [Video]. YouTube. https://www.youtube.com/watch?v=0Bz4-1YKI1M

This song shares six questions to keep in mind when reading and writing: *who*, *what*, *when*, *where*, *how*, and *why*.

Nick Jr. (n.d.). *Dora the explorer.* http://www.nickjr.com/dora-the-explorer

This site has links to episodes in the animated television series about Dora, a 7-year-old Latina girl, her talking purple backpack, and her monkey Boots, as they solve mysteries and engage in other explorations.

Scratch Garden. (2013). *The five W's song | English songs | Scratch garden* [Video]. YouTube. https://www.youtube.com/watch?v=vXWK1-L41f0

This catchy, country-style song explains the role of the five W questions in a story. In a surprise ending, H for How joins in.

TheBazillions. (2018). *"Who, What, When, Where, Why" by the Bazillions* [Video]. YouTube. https://www.youtube.com/watch?v=Y_E-N5y1r7g

The question words are cast in a song illustrated by a cartoon animation.

Other Inquiry Words Starting With W

▸ Ways of doing and knowing
▸ Ways to evaluate

‣ Weight in evaluation (e.g., for active participation, learning how to inquire in a discipline, thinking processes, social and cognitive strategies in solving ill-structured problems)

‣ Words (e.g., "in my own words. . .")

Connections

This chapter is especially related to *B is for Beginning*, *E is for Evidence*, *H is for Hypothesis*, *Q is for Questions*, and *S is for Sharing*.

Further Reading

AdLit.org. (n.d.). *Question-answer relationship (QAR)*. http://www.adlit.org/strategies/19802

Dennis-Shaw, S. (n.d.). *Lesson Plan. Guided comprehension: Self-questioning using question-answer relationships*. ReadWriteThink. http://www.readwritethink.org/classroom-resources/lesson-plans/guided-comprehension-self-questioning-227.html

Hu, H.-W., Chiu, C.-H., & Chiou, G.-F. (2019). Effects of question stem on pupils' online questioning, science learning, and critical thinking. *The Journal of Educational Research, 112*(4), 564–573. https://doi.org/10.1080/00220671.2019.1608896

Jones, R. C. (n.d.). *Strategies for reading comprehension: Question-answer relationships*. Reading Quest. https://www.readingquest.org/qar.html

King, A. (1992). Comparison of self-questioning, summarizing, and notetaking-review as strategies for learning from lectures. *American Educational Research Journal, 29*(2), 303–323. https://doi.org/10.3102/00028312029002303

X is for X

The letter *X* on its own should be neutral. But it isn't. X has many important meanings, positive and negative. Positively, X can be used to vote, choose a reply on a survey or test, signal a pedestrian-crossing zone, represent a variable in a mathematical equation, indicate the treasure's location on a pirate map, mark one's signature, substitute for a multiplication sign (actually ×) or the chi symbol (actually χ) in the common abbreviation for Christmas, or just be a mystery. Negatively, there is no mystery when X is penciled in red on students' work: The message is "This is wrong!"

Making X Happen

Educational psychology classes sometimes explore the scenario of a stressed parent trying to instill good manners while providing weekend breakfast to two children:

Parent to Child 1: *(child 2 watching from behind)* What do you want for breakfast?

Child 1: Gimme some of those darn cornflakes.

Parent: Don't talk to me that way! No breakfast; go to your room.

Parent to Child 2: *(hoping the example was set)* Now, what do you want for breakfast?

Child 2: For sure don't gimme any of those darn cornflakes!

This example makes two points: one simple and one more subtle. First, punishment, even observed rather than personally experienced, leads to avoidance. It does not teach what the parent or teacher intended. Child 2 focused on the cornflakes, not the rudeness. Seeing another child punished can be as impactful to the child who witnesses the punishment. Second, the example emphasizes that punishment is not the same as negative reinforcement. Reinforcement in teaching is a good thing; it removes a potential punishment or barrier to learning. Child 1 was punished for "getting it wrong," and Child 2 experienced the punishment vicariously. This chapter is about removing the negative power of X from interfering with students' motivation and learning by ensuring that it is not used as a punishment. Teachers should work especially hard to create an environment that sustains inquiry participation and learning by removing the likelihood of threats leading to embarrassment, hazing, bullying, or being made to feel incompetent. Doing so provides negative reinforcers of learning and of willingness to engage in inquiry.

The X we especially ask you to reflect on is the one used to denote a wrong answer. Students do not automatically understand or focus on precisely what part of the answer was wrong. They might overgeneralize to the point of deciding they are unworthy and never able to get anything right. They definitely take it personally. Doing inquiry, at least initially, is often challenging enough for learners and teachers without them being distracted by fear that they will be evaluated at every step and risk a global X as their acknowledgment. Everyone needs space to fumble a bit without being judged. People do not learn nearly as much from mistakes without being encouraged and scaffolded to do tasks correctly.

An error can occur at any step of the complex processes typically entailed in participation in inquiry instruction, and an X on a student's products from inquiring ignores all of the steps that were done well. Usually, there is something—or a lot—correct or creative about the path to a wrong answer. When thinking about the goals (see *G is for Goals*) of doing inquiry, it helps to contemplate what information can be collected and provided to recognize and support success: What evidence indicates that a learner knows something, knows how they came to know it, or knows how to learn new things? What evidence indicates that a teacher has taken the best approach? What information can be collected and used to show that inquiry is starting or working well in the classroom? What are the barriers that might be holding a student back from being highly motivated and learning effectively?

We much prefer concentrating on things done well, praising effort, and giving detailed feedback on work. During inquiry teaching, an appreciative smile and saying, "thank you," and "yes" to students' efforts are part of this list. It is okay for students to give a partial answer that shows some learning. When students leave something out, this does not automatically deserve a reprimand. Some students prefer, at least initially, to respond privately and not face a potentially critical audience. Students can do a trial run, for example, asking high-level questions, and self-evaluate their practice. Students working in groups can be guided to respond to each other in these same respectful, supportive ways, so they become part of the total classroom culture. Teachers can also remind students that "ex" is the opening sound of some wonderful words, such as *exact, excellent, exceed, exceptional, exchange, exciting, exhilarating, exotic, expert, extol, extra, extraordinary, extreme, exuberant,* and *exultant.* X is also the Roman numeral for 10; that's a 10! Students can extend or expand the list. Or teachers and students can adapt or choose a new word each day to use when giving feedback on inquiry participation.

Why X is Important

X can hurt. It has been widely used to denote errors, without offering at least clues about what is wrong or instructions for improvement. Punishment teaches avoidance, not the goal of the lesson, which is active or enthusiastic participation. The goal should be to build motivation, skills, and knowledge to support teachers' and students' engagement in inquiry. Teachers get more bang for their buck when they avoid X as a grading tool. Instead, support positive and meaningful forms of feedback.

See X in Action

AITSL. (2017). *Effective feedback animation* [Video]. YouTube. https://www.you tube.com/watch?v=LjCzbSLyIwI

This animation explains the research on effective feedback connected to setting goals and collecting evidence about learner performance, as well as different contributors of feedback.

Care.com. (2017). *What is negative reinforcement? | Care.com* [Video]. YouTube. https://www.youtube.com/watch?v=I6sU1rgcA9U

Negative reinforcement is not the same as punishment; it removes something negative, such as a barrier to the desired outcome. Four examples are house chores, eating, homework, and sleeping on time, but the idea applies equally to classroom teaching and learning.

Lerner, T. (2012). *Critique and feedback – The story of Austin's butterfly – Ron Berger* [Video]. YouTube. https://www.youtube.com/watch?v=hqh1MRW Zjms

A Maine classroom experiences how successive rounds of constructive feedback from a caring teacher helped first grader Austin improve his drawing of a butterfly. The teacher elicits and acknowledges students' input (i.e., uptake) as they engage in giving specific suggestions to improve the drawings and then review how to give positive feedback.

OER4Schools. (2013). *Shirley Clarke video on feedback* [Video]. YouTube. https://www.youtube.com/watch?v=DGNp0AJte_c

The video addresses positive ways to evaluate. The second half shows 10-year-olds engaged in formative peer assessment.

Other Inquiry Words Starting With X

There might not be any! Scrabble players know the challenge of finding English words that start with X. Here are a few related to inquiry that start with the sound "ex" if not the actual letter X:

▸ Ex (as in former or previous; connecting past to new understanding)
▸ Examine
▸ Example

- Exchange
- Exhibit
- Expect
- Explain
- Expo (a collection to display)

Connections

This chapter is especially related to *G is for Goals* and *V is for Valuing*.

Further Reading

Cameron, W. B. (1963). *Informal sociology: A casual introduction to sociological thinking*. Random House.

Zhuang, Y., Feng, W., & Liao, Y. (2017). Want more? Learn less: Motivation affects adolescents learning from negative feedback. *Frontiers in Psychology, 8*(76). https://doi.org/10.3389/fpsyg.2017.00076

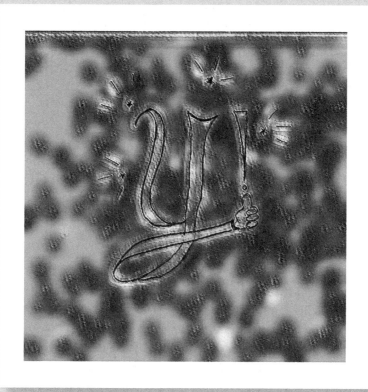

Y is for Yikes!

Inquiry instruction is full of surprises. Many of these surprises are positive, such as learning how much students can indeed take control of their learning, how eager they can be about complex and extended learning adventures, and how effectively they can help each other learn. Other kinds of inquiry surprises reflect learning challenges for some students. These call upon teachers' reflection, patience, adaptability, and sometimes special skills. For example, learners from time to time lack specific literacy, mathematical, or Internet skills associated with conducting thorough inquiry. Sometimes students need teacher guidance for literacy skills such as identifying main ideas in resource texts. Teacher coaching can help excitable or uncooperative students to select and practice appropriate social and ethical behavior. "Yikes!" announces that someone is surprised, and the "someone" can be the teacher, the student, or any of us.

Making Yikes! Happen

What are some of the surprises encountered in inquiry-based instruction?

Surprise #1. Inquiry success is contagious. Cheryl taught grade 7 language arts, history, and science. During an interview, she told us:

> My students were amazed but delighted when not only their grades in language arts improved, but so did their grades in social studies due to the new organizational skills needed in writing reports for general science. Students learned to plan, then draft, then edit, all before writing their final copy of their essay draft. The instruction guided them to understand how these strategies for writing would lead to greater success and that writing should play a role in several different subjects.

Although details of the inquiry process and what counts as evidence vary, many inquiry skills apply across subjects. Teachers can tell students about these connections, but students sometimes figure it out themselves. Bravo!

Surprise #2. Elementary students are typically less able to read and write informational prose well as compared to narratives. Students improve dramatically when teachers directly teach them to recognize main points, find topics and subtopics, and write summaries in their own words. All are relevant. How do teachers recognize this deficiency? Instead of paraphrasing and summarizing, students needing help often copy large chunks of text word-for-word. Such students also do not effectively separate important from irrelevant information or recall the gist of a text. Sometimes they bring too little relevant knowledge to make sense of the big ideas, or the material is beyond the text difficulty they can read fluently. They need to ask themselves, "What is this text saying?" and try to answer in their own words. This is a prime opportunity for teachers to monitor skills and chat with selected students to dispel current misconceptions. Students should read every selection twice—first to establish the main idea, and then to write notes. They will likely protest because most think that a good reader has to read anything only once. Research absolutely refutes this (especially the impact of rereading on reading fluency, well summarized by the report of the National Reading Panel [2000]).

Surprise #3. Students can spontaneously cover more curriculum content than teachers plan. An example in *E is for Evidence* described students who took photographs around the school related to a forthcoming ecology unit. Their class presentations covered every topic the teacher expected to introduce. A common teacher concern is that inquiry is inefficient and risks taking time from content coverage; again, this is refuted by the research evidence (see the Further Reading for examples).

Surprise #4. Inquiry can be a bumpy road. In *N is for Negotiating*, we described a working group that disintegrated. Perhaps some of the students needed to build trust and social skills useful to participating in inquiry before forming new teams for extended periods. When choosing teams comprising friends, students need to ensure that no one is left out. Disagreements are normal and can be productive. However, students also need practice disagreeing respectfully and separating the importance of content from the persons. At times, students should be asked to take the perspective of those with whom they disagree and later share how they felt about it. Formal debating or switching sides midway in dialogue can be useful. Periodically, invite students to try to switch an initial story interpretation, write it down, and later share with classmates how they felt about it.

Surprise #5. We asked science fair participants where they got their project ideas. A quarter replied that they got them from parents or science fair project books—so far not terrible—but some data were fabricated! They honestly reported cheating. The students took these shortcuts when they felt pressured to produce, timelines were short, and they felt they received insufficient teacher support. Even professional scientists have cheated (e.g., about "cold fusion") and offered parallel excuses. Teachers can take time at each stage to provide students encouragement and help them avoid pressure, especially with high-stakes situations, such as when facing public presentations.

Surprise #6. All people are web-dependent, but the Internet is not a safe place for a child to explore alone. Web blockers and filters at school protect students from some dark sites, but students might also search at home or a friend's house. We suggest taking the time, when brainstorming, to also discuss where to find new information. It is appropriate to limit searches to approved sources and to direct students to browse at home with a parent. Modeling, demonstrating, and practicing in class can help students internalize good search strategies.

Surprise #7. Students are sometimes fluent with familiar technology but much less savvy about using it creatively. A simple example we found was always using the same web browser rather than checking if the different search algorithms of other browsers might locate alternative information. Modern software can also help present information creatively in tables, charts, and graphs.

Why Yikes! is Important

Surprises are always present in inquiry, as both facilitators of and barriers to inquiry. A frequent source of surprise is when a mismatch arises between the learner's literacy or social communication skills and the demands faced during the inquiry process. Other surprises arise from uncertainty in the classroom learning environment or a gap between the planned and experienced lesson. Teachers can try to anticipate different surprises, both facilitators and barriers, so that every surprise is not Yikes! Sometimes the surprise is simply that students learned something different from what they set out to learn or more than the teacher expected them to learn.

See Yikes! in Action

Edutopia. (2017). *Cranking teaching strategies up to awesome* [Video]. YouTube. https://www.youtube.com/watch?v=A97RBq32kls

A school uses surprise, delight, and novelty as core instructional and curricular strategies.

Vancouver Public Schools. (2013). *The changing role of school librarians* [Video]. YouTube. https://www.youtube.com/watch?v=2dy3xQgsi1o

Modern teacher-librarians in Vancouver, British Columbia, explain where to find new information on the computer for learners with limited access to technology and show how to use this newfound information creatively.

Other Inquiry Words Starting With Y

‣ Yes
‣ Yin and yang

Connections

This chapter is especially related to *B is for Beginning, C is for Collaborating, E is for Evidence, K is for Knowledge, N is for Negotiating, P is for Process, R is for Roles, S is for Sharing,* and *U is for Uncertainty.*

Further Reading

Belfatti, M. A. (2012). *Contesting nonfiction: Fourth graders making sense of words and images in science information book discussions* [Unpublished doctoral dissertation]. University of Pennsylvania.

Hall, L. A. (2004). Comprehending expository text: Promising strategies for struggling readers and reading disabilities? *Reading Research and Instruction, 44*(2), 75–95.

Lodge, J., M., Kennedy, G., Lockyer, L., Arguel, A., & Pachman, M. (2018). Understanding difficulties and resulting confusion in learning: An integrative review. *Frontiers in Education, 3*(49). https://doi.org/10.3389/feduc.2018.00049

Lynette, R. (n.d.). *Teaching kids to paraphrase, step by step.* Minds in Bloom. https://minds-in-bloom.com/teaching-kids-to-paraphrase-step-by-step

McKibbon, S. (2016). The ins and outs of academic help seeking. *ASCD Education Update, 58*(12). https://www.ascd.org/publications/newsletters/education-update/dec16/vol58/num12/The-Ins-and-Outs-of-Academic-Help-Seeking.aspx

National Reading Panel. (2000). *Teaching children to read: An evidence-based assessment of the scientific research literature on reading and its implications for reading instruction.* National Institute of Child Health and Human Development. https://www.nichd.nih.gov/sites/default/files/publications/pubs/nrp/Documents/report.pdf

Power Up What Works. (n.d.). *Summarizing: Capture main ideas and details.* https://powerupwhatworks.org/sites/default/files/Lesson%20in%20Action%20-%20Summarizing%20-%20Capture%20Main%20Idea%20and%20Details.pdf

Shore, B. M., Aulls, M. W., & Delcourt, M. A. B. (Eds.). (2008). *Inquiry in education: Overcoming barriers to successful implementation* (Vol. 2). Routledge.

Teig, N., Scherer, R., & Nilsen, T. (2019). I know I can, but do I have the time? The role of teachers' self-efficacy and perceived time constraints in implementing cognitive-activation strategies in science. *Frontiers in Psychology, 10,* 1697. https://doi.org/10.3389/fpsyg.2019.01697

Z is for ZPD

Everyone seeks a bridge to connect what they currently know and what they need to know to accomplish a goal. The zone of proximal development (ZPD) theorized by Russian psychologist Lev Vygotsky (1978) represents the gap between what a learner can do without help and what they are close (proximal) to being able to achieve with guidance and encouragement from someone more knowledgeable. Eventually being able to do the task independently depends on the teacher's general ability to specifically scaffold the learning. A scaffold provides levels of temporary support that help students progressively become more competent in new inquiry, literacy, and curriculum content knowledge, skills, and strategies, and reduces the negative emotions and self-perceptions that some students might experience.

Making the ZPD Happen

The ZPD is there, whatever teachers do. We strongly support scaffolding instruction to help learners create new meaning. Scaffolding is a prime teacher tool in a constructivist classroom. Ongoing formal and informal monitoring of student progress is how teachers recognize what students can do unaided. Students faltering or requesting help on a new task is a cue that they need help taking the next step. In *T is for Talk Time*, we mentioned a teacher who asked students to ask two other peers before asking her for help. Once the learner masters the new task, the supports can be moved forward, like moving the yard markers when a North American football team earns a first down.

Scaffolding inquiry entails gradually increasing the complexity, difficulty, or sophistication of phases of the inquiry cycle (i.e., identifying a research topic, searching, collecting information or evidence, analyzing information, concluding, and communicating results). Teachers need many lessons to scaffold student learning through an inquiry project. The following paragraphs share some ways to construct scaffolds with students.

Scaffold #1. Clearly describe the goal of an inquiry activity or project, and then divide it into a series of mini-lessons. Division into subgoals, or subordinate learning events, should be done orally. Pace the events so that students can show by their actions and products that they are following the process. For example, a challenging arithmetic problem could be divided into several parts that are taught successively. Student learning is evaluated between each mini-lesson through both teacher- and student-initiated verbal discussion questions.

Scaffold #2. Develop the idea and skill of self-checking. When reading a story or a news clip as students follow along, pause periodically to ask inferential questions that you answer or ask a student to answer. Alter this activity by preparing three questions: (a) to check what the story seems to be about, (b) to check what important events have occurred, and (c) to ask for a summary at the end. Each of these three pauses ask students to self-check their understanding of the story so far. After each kind of reading, chat with students about the value of monitoring their understanding or memory and what to do if they realize they do not remember something. Later, when collecting information for a report on a topic or to answer a research question, check understanding by asking students to work in pairs to help each other read and self-check the same information resource.

Scaffold #3. Describe or illustrate a concept, problem, or process in two or three different ways. Illustrate orally with examples and metaphors. Model thinking aloud, by pantomime, or by demonstration. Use visual aids or pause to ask students to illustrate the concept by a drawing. After using preorganizers such as these, ask advanced learners to articulate in writing the illustrated concept, problem, or process in their own words. This task offers practice for students and gives the teacher evidence about who understands and what is understood.

Scaffold #4. Provide multiple sensory opportunities to acquire information as students carry out data collection. For example, show them how to study and remember features of a map visually, orally, and kinesthetically. This increases the likelihood of students remembering information. It also can be fun and empowering.

Scaffold #5. Offer students an example or model of an assignment they will complete. Describe the key features of the example and why the specific elements represent high-quality work. This cues students to know what to look for. A model provides a concrete example, usually visual and oral, of the learning outcomes to be achieved. Similarly, we might model a process (e.g., the procedures of a multistep science experiment), so that students can see what to do and how it is done before they try it themselves. Teachers could also ask a competent student to do the modeling or play the role of the team coach for the day.

Scaffold #6. Explain why learners are being asked to complete an assignment and how it will be evaluated. An explanation actually saves time because students become more aware of what is and is not important to complete within the assignment, more motivated, and less likely to experience frustration or give up.

Scaffold #7. Explicitly describe, before and after, how the new lesson builds on or connects to students' prior knowledge and skills from a previous lesson. A concept map can help—the students might work in teams to prepare this. Show and discuss with learners how the concepts and skills they already learned will likely help them with the new assignment or project. The teacher might also connect the lesson and the personal interests and experiences of the students. For example, in a history lesson, have a class discussion about a field trip to a museum at which students take notes or photos; this can take place before or after a unit in which students discuss specific events, persons, or artifacts.

Scaffold #8. Preview critical vocabulary before students read a difficult or unfamiliar text. Select the words most likely to challenge students using metaphors, analogies, or word-image associations; finding rhymes; using the words in sentences; and brainstorming synonyms, antonyms, and homonyms (words they might like to play with). When students then read the assignment, they will have greater confidence in their reading ability and interest in the content, and will more likely comprehend and remember the reading.

Scaffold #9. Provide clear directions. A written handout with step-by-step instructions guides students to take on a new challenge. Slowly adjust the scaffold by replacing the handout with a wall poster they can check when needed. Even kindergarten nonreaders can use a chart as a cue to remember what was said, especially if the teacher points to it each time they highlight a step. Later, students in small groups can write the instructions in their own words. Older students can use the guide or rubric that the teacher, or they, will use to evaluate their work.

Why the ZPD is Important

The idea of the ZPD helps teachers draw a map toward effective learning. It aids locating small learning gains in the context of larger objectives. Scaffolding for learning is intended to be temporary. After doing several inquiry projects, most students can take more responsibility for each phase of the process, initially under direct instruction and facilitation, and then as small groups working collaboratively.

See the ZPD in Action

687moo. (2014). *Zone of proximal development* [Video]. YouTube. https://www.youtube.com/watch?v=7Im_GrCgrVA

This animated video gives a summary of Vygotsky and his concept of zone of proximal development: what children can accomplish on their own and what they can accomplish with the help of another—whether a parent, teacher, or peer.

Asimow, J. (2013). *Puzzles and the zone of proximal development*. Math at Home. https://mathathome.org/puzzles-and-the-zone-of-proximal-development

This explanation features two short videos with kindergarten students. Each video shows a good example of the ZPD.

Bcb704. (2012). *Vygotsky's zone of proximal development* [Video]. YouTube. https://www.youtube.com/watch?v=0BX2ynEqLL4

This narrated summary of Vygotsky's ZPD show how children develop and learn by interacting with their environment. It includes photos of Vygotsky and modern classrooms.

Drmpcfl. (2010). *ZoneOfProximalDev.mov* [Video]. YouTube. https://www.you
tube.com/watch?v=Zu-rr2PRNkE

After brief narration, this video shows students helping each other as they work on assignments. The teacher demonstrates effective scaffolding as she helps learners understand and define their immediate tasks.

LBCC Learning Innovation Center. (2009). *Scaffolding language development* [Video]. YouTube. https://www.youtube.com/watch?v=gLXxcspCeK8

Teachers and students in pre-Kindergarten and primary classrooms demonstrate many forms of scaffolding.

Other Inquiry Words Starting With Z

▸ Zeal
▸ Zone (being in the zone)

Connections

This chapter is especially related to *A is for Activity*, *D is for Dialogue*, *F is for Facilitating*, *P is for Process*, and *R is for Roles*.

Further Reading

Alber, R. (2014). *6 scaffolding strategies to use with your students*. Edutopia. https://www.edutopia.org/blog/scaffolding-lessons-six-strategies-rebecca-alber

Belbase, S. (2014). Radical versus social constructivism: An epistemological-pedagogical dilemma. *International Journal of Contemporary Educational Research, 1*(2), 98–112. http://ijcer.net/en/download/article-file/147931

Culatta, R. (2011). *Zone of proximal development*. Innovative Learning. https://www.innovativelearning.com/educational_psychology/development/zone-of-proximal-development.html

Diefendorff, J. M., & Lord, R. G. (2008). Goal-striving and self-regulation processes. In R. Kanfer, G. Chen, & R. D. Pritchard (Eds.), *Work motivation: Past, present, and future* (pp. 151–196). Routledge.

Graham, K. (n.d.). *Howto: Scaffolding summary writing*. Busy Teacher. https://busyteacher.org/12282-scaffolding-summary-writing-how-to.html

Lajoie, S. P. (2005). Extending the scaffolding metaphor. *Instructional Science, 33*(5–6), 541–557. https://doi.org/10.1007/s11251-005-1279-2

McLeod, S. (2019). *What is the zone of proximal development?* Simply Psychology. https://www.simplypsychology.org/Zone-of-Proximal-Development.html

Osewalt, G. (n.d.). *Common advance organizers and why they work.* Understood. https://www.understood.org/en/school-learning/partnering-with-childs-school/instructional-strategies/common-advance-organizers-and-why-they-work

Pressley, M., Johnson, C. J., Symons, S., McGoldrick, J. A., & Kurita, J. A. (1989). Strategies that improve children's memory and comprehension of text. *The Elementary School Journal, 90*(1), 3–32. https://doi.org/10.1086/461599

Rosenshine, B., & Meister, C. (1992). The use of scaffolds for teaching higher-level cognitive strategies. *Educational Leadership, 49*(7), 26–33. https://www.ascd.org/ASCD/pdf/journals/ed_lead/el_199204_rosenshine.pdf

Sedita, J. (2019). *Scaffolds to support summarizing.* Keys to Literacy. https://www.keystoliteracy.com/blog/scaffolds-support-summarizing

Vygotsky, L. S. (1978). *Mind in society* (Trans. M. Cole). Harvard University Press.

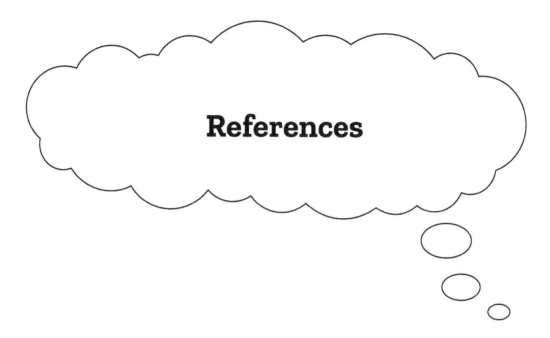

References

Anderson, L., & Krathwohl, D. R. (Eds.). (2001). *A taxonomy for learning, teaching, and assessing: A revision of Bloom's taxonomy of educational objectives* (Complete ed.). Longman.

Barfurth, M. A., & Shore, B. M. (2008). White water during inquiry learning: Understanding the place of disagreements in the process of collaboration. In B. M. Shore, M. W. Aulls, & M. A. B. Delcourt (Eds.), *Inquiry in education: Overcoming barriers to successful implementation* (Vol. 2, pp. 149–164). Routledge.

Bruner, J. S. (1977). *The process of education: A landmark in educational theory.* Harvard University Press. (Original work published 1960)

Challenging Learning. (2015). *James Nottingham's learning challenge (learning pit) animation* [Video]. YouTube. https://www.youtube.com/watch?v=3IMUAOhuO78

Csikszentmihalyi, M. (1990). *Flow: The psychology of optimal experience.* Harper & Row.

Dewey, J. (1902). *The child and the curriculum.* The University of Chicago Press.

Dewey, J. (1916). *Democracy and education: An introduction to the philosophy of education.* Macmillan.

Dewey, J. (1938). *Experience and education.* Macmillan.

Grow Waitaha. (2017). *Play-based learning (and inquiry)–supporting learner agency: Part 3* [Video]. YouTube. https://www.youtube.com/watch?v=UV212W8Ln-4

Lakatos, I. (1976). *Proofs and refutations: The logic of mathematical discovery.* Cambridge University Press.

Lave, J., & Wenger, É. (1991). *Situated learning: Legitimate peripheral participation.* Cambridge University Press.

Lim, J. (2010). *Strategies for building reading comprehension.* Scholastic. https://www.scholastic.com/teachers/blog-posts/justin-lim/reading-and-thinking-strategies-for-building-reading-comprehension

Locke, E. A., & Latham, G. P. (2006). New directions in goal-setting theory. *Current Directions in Psychological Science, 15*(5), 265–268. https://doi.org/10.1111/j.1467-8721.2006.00449.x

McLuhan, M. (1960). Classroom without walls. In E. Carpenter & M. McLuhan (Eds.), *Explorations in communications: An anthology* (pp. 1–3). Beacon Press.

Morisano, D., Hirsh, J. B., Peterson, J. B., Pihl, R. O., & Shore, B. M. (2010). Setting, elaborating, and reflecting on personal goals improves academic performance. *Journal of Applied Psychology, 95*(2), 255–264. https://doi.org/10.1037/a0018478

National Reading Panel. (2000). *Teaching children to read: An evidence-based assessment of the scientific research literature on reading and its implications for reading instruction.* National Institute of Child Health and Human Development. https://www.nichd.nih.gov/sites/default/files/publications/pubs/nrp/Documents/report.pdf

Pearson, P. D., Roehler, L. R., Dole, J. A., & Duffy, G. G. (1992). Developing expertise in reading comprehension. In S. J. Samuels & A. E. Farstrup (Eds.), *What research has to say about reading instruction* (2nd ed., pp. 145–199). International Reading Association.

Piaget, J. (1954). *The construction of reality in the child* (Trans. M. Cook). Basic Books.

Rowe, M. (n.d.). *The battle for the orange.* Compasito. http://www.eycb.coe.int/compasito/chapter_4/pdf/4_30.pdf

Saunders-Stewart, K. S., Walker, C. L., & Shore, B. M. (2013). How do parents and teachers of gifted students perceive group work in classrooms? *Gifted and Talented International, 28*(1–2), 99–106. https://doi.org/10.1080/15332276.2013.11678406

Schulman, M. (1993). Great minds start with questions: Practical ways to enhance your child's natural ability to think and create. *Parents, 68*(9), 99–102.

Shore, B. M., Aulls, M. W., & Delcourt, M. A. B. (Eds.). (2008). *Inquiry in education: Overcoming barriers to successful implementation* (Vol. 2). Routledge.

Spector, B. S., & Gibson, C. (1991). A qualitative study of middle school students' perceptions of factors facilitating the learning of science: Grounded theory and existing theory. *Journal of Research in Science Teaching, 28*(6), 467–484. https://doi.org/10.1002/tea.3660280603

Vygotsky, L. S. (1978). *Mind in society: The development of higher psychological processes* (Trans. M. Cole). Harvard University Press.

About the Authors

Bruce M. Shore has a B.Sc., teaching diploma, and M.A. (Education) from McGill University, and a Ph.D. (Educational Psychology) from The University of Calgary. A licensed teacher and psychologist, he has served as a mathematics teacher, educational psychology professor, department chair, President of the McGill Association of University Teachers, Dean of Students, and now Professor Emeritus. His scholarship explores inquiry-based teaching and learning and able students' cognition and social thinking. He is a National Association for Gifted Children Distinguished Scholar, was listed among the "53 most influential people in gifted education," and shared six Mensa International Awards for Excellence in Research in human intelligence and intellectual giftedness. He received McGill's Faculty of Education Distinguished Teaching Award, the David Thomson Award for Excellence in Graduate Supervision and Teaching, and the Principal's Prize for Excellence in Teaching, as well as the Canadian Committee for Graduate Students in Education Mentorship Award. He authored or coauthored more than 225 books, chapters, articles, and reports, and is a Fellow of the American Educational Research Association. He is McGill Chapter Co-Advisor of the Golden Key International Honour Society and its International Leadership Council Secretary.

Mark W. Aulls has a B.S. (Education) from Ball State University, an M.A. (Reading Education) from Indiana, and an Ed.D. (Reading) from the University of Georgia. Previously a junior high school English teacher and reading consultant, he is Professor Emeritus of Educational Psychology at McGill University. He is the author of three books for teaching reading in elementary school and coauthor of three books on inquiry education. Professor Aulls was the first author of two published literacy programs for elementary school: *QUEST New Roads to Literacy* and *Active Composing and Teaching*. His published research has focused on reading comprehension strategies, classroom processes and their correspondence to learning and to students' perceptions of instruction, the nature of teacher-student dialogue and its influence on student learning, the qualitative study of educator perceptions of inquiry and inquiry instruction, and mixed-model research on inquiry-based instruction in elementary, middle, and university classrooms. He was a member of the Center for the Study of Learning and Performance at Concordia University and team leader for its Scientific Reasoning and Inquiry Group. Professor Aulls is the Past President of the Montreal Reading Association and a member of the board of directors for the National Reading Conference, and was a Fellow at the Center for the Study of Reading.

Diana Tabatabai started her career as a chemist in Tehran, Iran, with a B.Sc. (Chemistry) before coming to Canada and receiving her M.A. (Educational Planning) from the Ontario Institute for Studies in Education at the University of Toronto. She worked as an instructional technology consultant at the Toronto Board of Education before moving to Montreal, where she became a part-time elementary school teacher before pursuing her passion to find ways that empower and engage learners in inquiry-driven classrooms. She earned her Ph.D. in educational psychology at McGill University and became part of the research team as a research associate visiting schools, encouraging teachers to adopt inquiry teaching, and jointly publishing research on inquiry-based learning and teaching.

Juss Kaur Magon received her B.Sc. (Chemistry) from Concordia University, diplomas in teaching and gifted education from McGill University, and an M.Sc. and D.Phil. (Educational Research) from Oxford University. She is an international education consultant and has successfully mentored more than 800 teachers in Saudi Arabia, United Arab Emirates, India, and Nigeria with Pearson Education and independently. Her expertise lies in the field of education for the gifted and inquiry-based teaching and learning strategies involving critical thinking skills and self-directed learning. Earlier in her career, Dr. Kaur Magon was a department head and teacher in mathematics and science at various secondary schools across England, the United States, and Canada. Over the years, Dr. Kaur Magon has been instrumental in the planning, implementation, and execution of several gifted programs, and is presently involved in an ongoing consultation and training of teachers in inquiry-based learning and teaching in India. Dr. Kaur Magon has been involved in inquiry-related research in the Department of Educational and Counselling Psychology at McGill University in Montreal, Canada, for a decade, where she was also an adjunct professor. Her in-depth experience in working at all levels of school life enables her to work very closely with school management and teachers to raise student achievement by motivating them intrinsically. Dr. Kaur Magon is also a visual artist. She has exhibited her work in Canada, Singapore, and London. Recently she published the book *Mantra Art: The Journey Within,* which is a compilation of all of her paintings.